Yeshua
OUR ATONEMENT

Derek Leman

Yeshua Our Atonement
By Derek Leman

ISBN 978-1508404040

First Edition 2012.
Create Space Edition February 2015
This book is printed on archival quality paper.

Table of Contents

BIBLIOGRAPHY

Boyarin, Daniel. 2012. *The Jewish Gospels: The Story of the Jewish Christ.* New York: The New Press.

Bruce, F.F. 1990. *The Epistle to the Hebrews (NICNT Commentary Series).* Grand Rapids: Eerdmans.

Friedman, Richard Elliott. 1987. *Who Wrote the Bible?* New York: HarperCollins.

McKnight, Scot. 2007. *A Community Called Atonement.* Nashville: Abingdon.

Milgrom, Jacob. 1991. *Leviticus 1–16 (The Anchor Bible).* New York: Doubleday.
— 2004. *Leviticus.* Minneapolis: Fortress.
— 1990. *The JPS Torah Commentary: Numbers.* Philadelphia, New York: Jewish Publication Society.

Soulen, R. Kendall. 1996. *The God of Israel and Christian Theology.* Minneapolis: Fortress.

Zuntz, Günther. 1946. *The Text of the Epistles: A Disquisition Upon the Corpus Paulinum: The Schweich Lectures of the British Academy 1946.* Reprint by Wipf & Stock, 2007.

Chapter 1
Beginning of a New Understanding

There are two basic ways to work on a theory of the meaning of Yeshua's atoning death. One way is to start with the cross and work backwards, re-reading the Hebrew Scriptures in light of certain ideas we may have about the cross. The other is, as much as possible, to read it forward– from the ideas of atonement in the Hebrew Scriptures to the cross.

This book is based on the second method. Books have been written many times before from the first method, with what I would argue are inaccurate results. The realization that Yeshua is our atonement came into being from a rich background. Yeshua came as the Messiah of Israel, so that it is difficult to imagine our task would be to erase the lessons of Torah about atonement and write over them a new theology. If Yeshua is not the apex of all the sacrificial symbolism of Israel's Tabernacle and Temple, then how is he Israel's Messiah?

The goal of this short volume is to illuminate the atonement of Yeshua for modern readers. The meaning of atonement moves forward from Torah (especially Leviticus) to Messiah. From the Day of Atonement to the sacrifices of the Temple to the strange purity laws of Leviticus, the trajectory of atonement builds in mystery and resolves itself in Messiah. Perhaps the clearest connecting point between the two is the book of Hebrews (concerning which the reader will find two chapters). The endpoint of atonement is much greater than a pleasant afterlife. It is the summing up of all things with perfect goodness in Messiah in a world to come where all sorrow is put away and joy commences for unending time. Not only people, but the very fabric of the universe is to be redeemed.

Insight from Unusual Places

My own perception of atonement was changed in stages. There were three influential passages of scripture: the parable of the Pharisee and tax collector in Luke's gospel, the Yom Kippur chapter of Leviticus, and two verses in the book of Hebrews. There were also one life-changing experience and two influential books. One of these books was by a Jewish scholar of the Hebrew Bible and the other by a Christian theologian.

The life-changing experience is also where the Pharisee and tax collector parable enters the picture. Here is how it happened. I was at an Orthodox Jewish synagogue on Yom Kippur. I didn't belong there. In fact, I was an invader, a Christian who felt Judaism was spiritually bankrupt. I was there to pray that these Jewish men and women would believe in Jesus and join a church like the one I attended.

Even with my limited understanding of the depth and beauty of Judaism at that time, I was awed by the skill required to worship in such a place. I was awed by the significance of the day. I didn't for a second believe anyone needed to keep Yom Kippur anymore (I simplistically believed that the atonement Yeshua made rendered a day like this obsolete). I felt as if I was back in time, witnessing an "Old Testament" event adapted to modern customs. It was, in that sense, the holiest day of the year. As I would later discover, Yom Kippur could be translated the "Day of Purgation" (as we will see in the next chapter).

So many elements of this service seemed wrong. They prayed pre-written prayers, liturgy which seemed so spiritually dead. Such thoughts betrayed my ignorance of the biblical examples such as Psalms and the Lord's Prayer, and the fact that many Protestants have a rich liturgy, such as Lutherans and Episcopalians. But even if I were knowledgeable I would have been certain that they were also completely missing God. My way was the right way, of course, and theirs was wrong. As an outside observer looking in on this service, I noticed that some of the men were on their knees, heads touching the floor in prostration. Others had their noses buried in prayer books and seemed to be concentrating intently. I was truly taken aback when some of the men started ritually beating their chest.

Mind you, I am not saying that the Yom Kippur custom is to pound one's chest with any serious force. It is a light movement of the fist, repeatedly into the chest, in rhythm with the prayer and it occurs only in certain parts of the service. In the Amidah prayer said three times daily, there is also a very brief beating of the chest. But on Yom Kippur this happens in a more extensive fashion.

I was nervous. My sense of being an intruder increased. I hoped to be overlooked, asked no questions. Fortunately for me, it being Yom Kippur and all, people were too busy praying to socialize or ask who I was. I had heard someone say, in a sermon about "saving the Jews," that the sign of chest-beating was tragic, the desperate action of a hopeless people seeking divine mercy apart from knowledge. I very much interpreted their action in this way.

Yet even before I left the room, I confess, I started to feel it. The spirit of group repentance was contagious. I also found myself praying about my own shortcomings. There was a spiritual power not only in the chest-beating, but in the act of touching the ground with the forehead. I didn't have the courage to join these synagogue members in either act, but I felt confused by a sense of admiration for what they were doing.

Sometime later I read Yeshua's parable, of the Pharisee and the tax collector, and my heart nearly stopped. The one Yeshua praised was the tax collector who beat his chest. The one Yeshua criticized was the one who felt spiritually superior.

I was not like the chest-beating tax collector, or the prostrating men who bowed before the open doors of the Ark in the synagogue sanctuary. I was like the Pharisee in Yeshua's parable, convinced that I had it and they didn't.

What did Yeshua say about the chest-beater? In the ESV translation we read, "I tell you, this man went down to his house justified, rather than the other" (Luke 18:14). The word "justified" is a good word in the evangelical circles I was part of. In our circles it meant "saved, going to heaven." In a more informed understanding it means "one declared in the right" in the courtroom of God.

That experience did two things for me. First, it made me seek out more information about Yom Kippur. I will discuss this at length in the next chapter ("Day of Purgation [Yom Kippur]"). Second, it made me question some of the "certainties" in my thinking about atonement. Would the Atoner himself really say that things like chest-beating are important in order to be justified by God? Did this fit with my automatic-atonement-by-mental-assent theory of the gospel?

Heavy Books and Obscure Rituals

My new-found interest in Yom Kippur led me to buy a book of more than 1,100 pages covering only sixteen chapters of what I figured had to be the least interesting book in the Bible. I am talking about the commentary on Leviticus by Jacob Milgrom (now available in the Anchor-Yale series). The size didn't frighten me away from buying the book since I planned only to read his comments on one chapter, Leviticus 16.

But as I read, the mysteries of Yom Kippur piled on instead of shrinking: scenes of priests dashing blood; the mercy seat ("atoning place" or "atonement cover") on the Ark; a veil between the rooms inside the shrine; priestly garments being changed; two goats; the use of the lot; Azazel and the scapegoat. I quickly determined that I would have to start at the beginning of Leviticus.

The more I read Milgrom, the more I realized his way of looking at things was very foreign to me. Some of it I chalked up to "he's just a liberal" (the self-superiority thing again, a big part of my religion). But much as I was inclined to find fault, a lot of his explanations made sense.

I read and re-read the section on Leviticus 1–4. I underlined things. Slowly I began to understand: the sacrifices in ancient Israel were not what I thought they were. Some of the books on my shelf about the Tabernacle and the offerings were very different in their approach. If I accepted what Milgrom was saying, my understanding of sacrifices would have to change.

I was just getting started. The next big realization would come concerning matters of cleanness and uncleanness (purity and impurity). These laws had always seemed strange to me (women have to purify themselves after having a baby?). Though I was more than a little overwhelmed with the detail in this commentary, I started to understand that the purity laws of Torah are not minor. They are crucial to understanding what atonement is about and why it is needed.

Where did the death of Messiah come into all of this? Jacob Milgrom, who died in 2010, was a conservative Jew. He did not correlate his commentary on Leviticus to theology about the death of Yeshua. How did the obscure rituals of the old Temple culture of Israel inform my understanding of Yeshua? After all, it was Yeshua who said, "Something greater than the Temple is here" (Matthew 12:6, ESV).

A Community Called Atonement

I had absorbed a fair amount of Jewish scholarship on Leviticus, but I needed to understand the story of Messiah's death more completely. I desired to comprehend the benefits that the death of Messiah could communicate to us as his followers. I started reading a blog by a professor who was then teaching at North Park University in Illinois. I found this professor had a book with "atonement" in the title.

In *A Community Called Atonement*, Scot McKnight asks and answers the most important practical question about all of this: does atonement work? That is, if we think something Messiah did affects radical change in people and in the universe, does it work and if so how does it work? Can we see evidence of it working? Does it work according to a plan that makes sense, one that is believable?

If atonement doesn't really work, then it doesn't matter much if I parse some ancient texts to discover the theory of atonement in Leviticus, in Daniel, in Hebrews, in Pauline letters, or in Revelation. How does Messiah's death work for us?

People have fought theological battles over such things throughout church history. The word "atonement" (which, in truth, is a made-up word and not directly related to any biblical word) has been variously defined. People have lost jobs and reputation over such matters. As McKnight states, "Atonement theories have been shaped by the history of atonement theories" (9). In other words, people have formed camps, assumed that one theory is best, and have rejected or downplayed other theories.

McKnight says this is all wrong and starts his book with an analogy from the game of golf. Atonement theories are like the different clubs in a golfer's bag. You bring them all to the game and you don't pick just one. Later he says atonement theories are like strings on a violin. The music can work with one string, but sounds fuller, richer, when all of the strings get involved.

Atonement, in its full sense of Messiah bringing all things together for perfection in the world to come (see chapter 10, "The Full Picture of Messianic Atonement"), is far more than God saying "presto" and making it happen. Atonement works from within; within a community of people who are changed by it, and within individuals who come into such communities to be changed.

It is far more than individual rescue or invitation to afterlife. It is Ephesians 1:10 (ESV), "a plan for the fullness of time, to unite all things in him." It is a transaction resulting in renewed people, renewed communities, a renewed earth, and a renewed cosmos.

I found out from Scot McKnight that the full picture of atonement is described primarily in five metaphors (see chapter 9, "Metaphors of Divine Atonement"). The work of atonement has been described in six different accomplishments of Messiah. We need all of the golf clubs, the full set of violin strings. Much is required to bring about the ideal world God is making.

Getting More "Hebrew"

So far I've told the story of a life-changing experience, the influence of one of Yeshua's parables, the book of Leviticus, Milgrom's commentary, and McKnight's book about atonement. The remaining insight was the New Testament book of Hebrews.

There are few books in the New Testament directed primarily at Messianic Jews (Jewish followers of Yeshua). One of them is Hebrews.

For a while I wasn't sure what to do with Hebrews. It seems like a book that challenges the idea of Judaism and calls people to come outside of Judaism to be with Yeshua (see Hebrews 13:11–13). People have used Hebrews to tell me and others that Judaism is of no value in Messiah. They say, and can use some verses in Hebrews to back it up, that Judaism was the old shadow which has now passed over the land and the new glorious way of Christianity has lit up the darkness to drive away the shadows.

But I have learned to trust that "Hebrews knows its stuff" (as I will explain in chapter 5). In particular, two verses in Hebrews seemed to confirm what I had learned from Leviticus and Milgrom. In the first one, the unknown genius behind Hebrews speaks about a lack in what the animal offerings of ancient Israel could do. This need not be read in any way as a criticism of God, the Torah, the Temple, or the animal offerings. It has a more important point. The animal offerings themselves point us to something beyond them, something that will do what we really need: "According to this arrangement, gifts and sacrifices are offered that cannot perfect the conscience of the worshiper" (Hebrews 9:9, ESV).

In the second one, much like the first, the writer of Hebrews again speaks of a lack in the animal offerings. There is a contrast between the death of Messiah and the death of a sacrificial victim in the Temple courts: "For it is impossible for the blood of bulls and goats to take away sins" (Hebrews 10:4, ESV). But don't we want an offering that will remove sins? Isn't that the hope of many scriptures ("You will hurl all our sins into the depths of the sea,"

(Micah 7:19, JPS)?

I found that the writer of Hebrews has a creative imagination but also a solid grasp of priestly details and mysteries. Not only does Hebrews "know its stuff," but it also profoundly explains the mysteries connecting Leviticus and Yeshua (see chapter 6, "Hebrews and Priestly Mysteries").

Atonement Matters

Atonement is like gravity. It is true whether or not you or I, or any particular person, comprehend what it is or how it works. So why learn about it? What difference does an understanding of atonement make?

It matters for those who ask the question, "Should I believe in Yeshua?" It is certainly true that people who read books about atonement are quite likely to be among the already convinced. Nonetheless, if the community of faith understands atonement, communication will improve with those who ask the hard questions. Perhaps the hardest is, "Why Yeshua?"

Atonement begins before Yeshua, but Yeshua is the center and end of atonement. The simple answer, "You need Yeshua to experience joy in the afterlife" is satisfactory for some. Many want to know more. For a Jewish person, to understand how the Torah is open-ended, implying that there is more to come in reconciling God and humanity than Torah alone provides, is vital. Judaism ends with questions which are expected to be answered by God. This study of atonement is intended to show how those questions are resolved and carried further by Yeshua in what has since been revealed. Of course there are new questions as Yeshua's atoning work brings our faith and hope in the direction of a redeemed cosmos.

For any person, life itself is open-ended, raising questions about what more is to come and what meaning present existence has. Atonement is about the "what more is to come" and is at least a theory that every person should consider. Does atonement theory carry along the questions of meaning and hope for healing that we all as humans have? Of course atonement theory does not answer all questions, and perhaps we should realize the future God has in store is endless. Yet it may be that understanding the all-encompassing, cosmos-healing work of Messiah will bring us to a higher level of faith and hope.

Atonement matters for those who believe in Yeshua and who need faith and hope. Faith raises questions. A fuller understanding of Yeshua's role as the center of all things answers some questions and gives hope concerning others. Hope looks toward the good we trust God to prepare for us. Atonement fills in that hope with many colors shining brightly.

Atonement matters for those who believe in Yeshua who might not comprehend how central Yeshua is to everything. We get lost in the details. Serving can become central. The forms in which we worship can become central. Doctrinal do's and don'ts can become central. Atonement is a grand study of the potent healing work of God and at the center of everything is Messiah. Returning to the center, placing all faith and hope in Messiah so that our love flows through Messiah to the world, is finding the peace and wisdom of God. The other important matters of faith and hope, like serving and beliefs and forms, will all flow better from the center.

Atonement matters for those who are asking the question, "How should I live?" As the title of Scot McKnight's book indicates, atonement is to be worked out in communities, in congregations of imperfect people sharing faith and hope. McKnight makes the daring statement, which is best understood by those who realize how deep and wide atonement really is, "Atonement is something done not only by God for us, but also something we do with God for others" (117).

God brings all things together for good. Subatomic particles respond to his call. The world of living things is all to be redeemed and all things, therefore, become servants as God beckons them. Yet his most concentrated system for redemption and renewal is circles of people, sharing the path of discipleship under Messiah. Atonement works in community.

Our individualistic cultures think that gathering with and befriending like-minded people of faith is a matter of lesser importance. This is not a book on ecclesiology (the name for the theological understanding of congregations). Yet atonement is a matter of faith to be shared between people committed to one another. The community of Yeshua has this message which is healing for those who come inside. While we wait for the great soul-transforming moments to come, in this present world, we have each other.

If anyone doubts that atonement is communal, they should ask, "Is the notion that congregations together form the 'body of Messiah' a meaningful or meaningless concept?" Messiah is at work today, not just in words written down thousands of years ago.

Chapter 2
Day of Purgation (Yom Kippur)

The right way to say it is Yom (rhymes with "dome") kee-POOR (accent is on the last syllable). Don't be surprised if you hear people pronounce it in the vernacular of American-Jewish as yomm (rhymes with "bomb") kipper (rhymes with "slipper").

The usual translation in English is "day of atonement," but that gets us into a couple of issues right from the start. First, atonement is not a biblical word. Second, the root meaning of "kippur" is wiping something away, cleansing something, or purging out something not desired. Thus, Jacob Milgrom calls it the Day of Purgation (1,009). And "purgation" refers to purification or cleansing, or even in some dictionaries a ceremonial cleansing from a state of defilement. Once you start to understand things like pollution, defilement, symbolic systems of purity laws (more detail to come in the "Ritual Pollution: Sin and Death" chapter) the word purgation makes more and more sense.

But this chapter on the Day of Purgation has enough mysteries already. It is about that enigmatic day on the Jewish calendar—on what used to be the Temple calendar—when the high priest went beyond the veil into the innermost room, where the Glory resided. The chapter on Yom Kippur is Leviticus 16 (or is it? See below). There are two goats, a ram, and a bull to consider. There are two types of sacrifices and one rite that are unlike anything else done in ancient Israel—the sending out of a live goat bearing on it the guilt of the people. There is the mystery of Azazel, a word subject to two longstanding possible interpretations. And there are other puzzles; not least is why the occasion of Yom Kippur is not even mentioned until verse 29.

After the Death

Leviticus 16 is the beginning of one of the weekly readings followed by Jews all over the world in cycling through the Torah year after year. The reading that covers Leviticus 16:1–18:30, is called *Akharei Mot*, "after the death." It is called that, quite simply, because verse 1 begins with those very words. The deaths in question are that of Aaron's two sons, the priests Nadab and Abihu, which occurred back in chapter 10.

Whatever we read in Leviticus 16 has something to do with death. It is part of the mystery of dying. But why does it come six chapters later than the deaths of these two sons of Aaron? What has come in between that terrible, double loss of life, which took place in the sacred courtyard, near the altar of burnt offering, and this chapter on the purging of the Holy Place?

The answer to what has come in between is simple: the laws of purity and impurity. Chapter 11 is about impure meat and contamination of pottery vessels. Chapter 12 is about impurity following childbirth. Chapters 13 and 14 are about a special issue of impurity concerning a biblical skin disease (often translated leprosy, but not the same as the disease we now call by that name). Chapter 15 is about gonorrhea and its discharges (not kidding!), emissions of semen, and menstruation. There is one other cause of impurity, but it is not discussed until much later, in Numbers 19: contact with a human corpse or even proximity to someone who has had contact with one.

To recap then, Leviticus 16 starts with the phrase "after the death" and it comes six chapters after the deaths of Nadab and Abihu. In between that incident and Leviticus 16 are the chapters on impurity, its causes, and its treatment. This all seems like a riddle to a modern reader. To the ancients it was not hard to see the connections. I will reveal more in a little while.

Tenth Day, Seventh Month

The holy month in the Hebrew Bible is the seventh month, which has, since the days of the Babylonian exile, been called Tishri. Seven is, of course, a symbolic number often used in scripture to designate something holy, something that pertains especially to God and his plan. This seventh month began with the sounding of a shofar (ram's horn, see Leviticus 23:23–25). Ten days later was the day set aside for purgation of the sanctuary called Yom Kippur (Leviticus 23:26–33). Five days after that began the great Feast (Tabernacles, aka Booths, in Hebrew, Sukkot, Leviticus 23:34–43). At this third observance in the seventh month the people dwell in brush arbors and celebrate at a great feast. The pattern is: warning – purgation – dwelling and feasting.

There is a certain order to the observances of the holiest month on the calendar. It is still reflected in Jewish customs in our time. The ten days between Rosh HaShanah (the day of shofar blasts) and Yom Kippur are a time for repentance and extra prayers. The seven days of Sukkot, plus the eighth day, are about rejoicing, gathering, and feasting. The pattern is preparation and repentance, purging of sin and death, and feasting in the light of the divine Presence.

But the relationship of Leviticus 16 to Yom Kippur is a conundrum (though not an unsolvable one). At this stage we should note: the tenth day of the seventh month is not even mentioned until verse 29. If Leviticus 16 is about Yom Kippur, why isn't the day mentioned until the end?

All of the instructions about the high priest, the two goats, the bringing of blood into the Holy Place behind the veil, sending out the live goat, and so on, are in the context of a reaction to death. Leviticus 16 is actually about something that must happen in response to a certain kind of death, a death that occurs in God's holy courts. As we will see, these are also the instructions for Yom Kippur. But first and foremost, the drastic steps taken in Leviticus 16 are God purging the pollution of death from his holy house. As Jacob Milgrom puts it, "the original form of the purgation rite described in verses 2–28 was an emergency measure invoked by the high priest whenever he felt that the entire sanctuary had to be purged" (1,061).

The Basic Steps of the Yom Kippur Temple Purging in Israel

Reading Leviticus 16 closely will render some surprises. Verse 16 is most telling, "he shall atone the Holy Place from the impurities of the people of Israel and from their transgressions, even all their sins" (my translation). Why does the inner room of the Temple need to have an atonement? Isn't atonement for people? How will this idea ever fit into an understanding of what God has done in Messiah to make atonement for us as a people? The mysteries of atonement are not impenetrable, but they may be deeper and richer than we have heard in simplistic theories. Maybe it is worth some concentration and a little effort to penetrate the veil and see the meaning of atonement.

When I first picked up Jacob Milgrom's commentary on Leviticus 1–16, I was dumbfounded. I didn't understand a tenth of what he was saying. But I have to admit I was fascinated.

Consider first the basic order of what the high priest does in the purgation ritual: he purifies himself, he purifies the Holy Place, he purifies the Tent itself, he transfers the people's guilt to a living goat, and he sends that guilt where it belongs: to the desert demons (Azazel is probably an old name for a goat demon and the use of this name no more implied a literal belief in goat demons than the Bible's use of Leviathan and Rahab imply belief in sea-monsters). Sending sin to demons? Purifying a building? Before we comment on the steps in more detail, let's consider a similar custom in Babylon.

The Babylonian Rite of Purging the Temple of Bel

At a garage sale in 1990, I saw a huge, orange book with a library cover (clear plastic) and a library label on it. The spine said *Ancient Near Eastern Texts Relating to the Old Testament*. I was a poor college student, newly married, with one child on the way. Our grocery budget was about $25 a week. The book was $50, but it had 735 pages of English translations and information about old Egyptian and Mesopotamian writings with relevance to the study of the Hebrew Bible. I remember asking my wife if we could live on bread and water for a week, so I could get this book. She said, "I know this is an investment in what you will do with your life." I don't think we actually had to eat bread and water that week, but it was a tough drain on our budget.

It was one of several turning points in my study of the Hebrew Bible, with the mentorship in my early training coming from Dr. John Walton, a leading scholar especially focused on Near Eastern contexts of the Hebrew Bible. I began to discover again and again something which might scandalize some readers of the Bible: nearly every custom in the Torah of Israel is related to similar customs in neighboring countries. Egyptians and Babylonians and Canaanites and Hittites had temples and sacrifices and purity laws and ceremonies too. If we read the Torah of Israel (Genesis–Deuteronomy) in ancient times, if we had lived during the centuries of the First Temple (950–586 BCE) or even the Second Temple (516 BCE–70 CE), we would see the connections naturally.

Yet in between their time and ours, a great deal of ignorance has crept in. Old ways have been forgotten. Cultural and historical context have become the province of scholars and academics. Religious readers of the Bible often choose to ignore the history, to pick at the surface meaning with no research into the way early hearers of the Bible would relate it to the culture and religious beliefs of people in their time.

The key to understanding many customs in Torah is how they differ from what other nations did.

In James Pritchard's *Ancient Near Eastern Texts Relating to the Old Testament* we find a text describing the Temple purging ceremony of the Babylonians at a certain period. Jacob Milgrom presents an updated translation in *Leviticus: A Book of Ritual and Ethics*. The highlights of the Babylonian ceremony include:

» *The month for the Babylonian ceremony is Nisannu. (On the Jewish calendar, Nisan is the month of Passover and is the new year for kings.)*

» *The Babylonian priest dons a white linen robe and enters the temple of Bel and Beltiya. (The Israelite high priest also wears white linen.)*

» *He purifies (atones for) the temple of Bel and Beltiya and then enters other temples to purify them.*

» *He sprinkles water from the Tigris and Euphrates on the temple building itself. (The Israelite high priest sprinkles goat's blood.)*

» *He smears (anoints) the temple doors with cedar oil. (Cedar wood features in several Torah rituals as it is red, the color of blood.)*

» *In the court he burns incense. (The Israelite high priest uses incense smoke as a protective screen to keep from being killed by God's Presence in the Holy Place.)*

» *He has a lower priest bring him a decapitated ram and uses the blood to purify the temple. (The Israelite priest used a slaughtered, not decapitated, male goat.)*

» *He throws the body of the ram into the river and takes the head into the desert. (The Israelite high priest sends a living goat into the desert.)*

» *The priest of Bel is quarantined from the temple precincts for seven days. (The priest who dispatches the living goat in Israel is impure until sundown.)*

» *He strikes the cheek of the Babylonian king, drags him by the ears, and makes him bow before Bel. (Israel has no comparable political humiliation ritual.)*

» *The king must cry tears or it is a bad omen.*

Jacob Milgrom summarizes the differences, which imply the different way in which God teaches Israel to understand atonement. In Babylon the main concern is demons. In Israel, the main concern is the relation between the people and God, into which sins and impurities insert themselves as barriers. In Babylon the source of the purifying blood (the ram) is eliminated (thrown into the river and desert) while in Israel the sins of the nation are eliminated. The Babylonian ram is more about keeping demons away, while in Israel the ritual is about keeping the Presence of God near to the people in spite of sin and death. The Babylonian ritual is also about religion and politics, the king being slapped and humiliated before their god. In Israel the issue is the people's relation to God, not the right of the priests to overrule the king. In essence, the Babylonian ritual is about the danger of demons, the necessity of religion to protect the people from harm, and the power of superstition. In Israel, the ritual is about the place where God meets with the people, and keeping it free from all pollution of sin and death.

The Strange Ways of Torah

The things we care about in modern life are in some ways different and in some ways the same as what concerned ancient people. Heavy on our modern list of concerns are things like entertainment and comfort. Heavy on the list of ancient concerns were survival, protection from demonic evil, and the continuation of the family line. Yet the differences should not be exaggerated. As strange as the rituals in Leviticus 16 or in the temple purgation ceremony in Babylon may look to us, we share their concern with things like: a good lot in life, the meaning of life and death, and the relation of humans to higher power(s) in the heavens.

In teaching Israel a different ritual of purging the Temple, God taught the people lessons about life, faith, and relating to him. The thing to be concerned about is not demons. The worry about unseen enemies, superstitious causes of catastrophe, of malevolent powers bringing death and suffering is not valid. God is in control of the forces of life and death. It is not that faith in God will prevent death and suffering, but it will create a trust that God will make "good" every harm suffered. The way to approach life is not to fear evil, but to trust the One who will somehow—and no explanation is offered about how it will all work—redeem suffering and bring an end to sin and death. The purity system in Israel, as we will see in coming chapters, is very much about sin and death.

When a human death occurs near God's Temple, there must be a purging. There is something wrong with death. The deaths of Nadab and Abihu are impure, threatening the departure of God from the Temple. It is a mystery how, at once, God could cause the deaths of Nadab and Abihu and, at the same time, despise that very death. It is a mystery how the death of animals, the use of their life-force (the blood), is involved in cleansing the impurity of death. This is more than a hint that death must be allowed, in the present time, to run its course, but that death is not the final word.

Leviticus 16:16 says that the high priest atones for the Holy Place and that he does so for two things: impurities (uncleannesses in some translations) and sins of the people. To better understand atonement, we should consider the Torah's theology about these three things: the meaning of the word atonement, the meaning of impurity, the meaning of sin.

To Atone: Not "to cover" but "to wipe away"

Misinformation about the meaning of atonement for the most part comes from Genesis 6:14. God tells Noah to *kafar* (cover) the Ark with *kofer* (pitch). Both words come from the Hebrew root kaf-peh-resh (k-p-r). The word for atoning, as in Leviticus 16, is *kiper* (from the same root, as "p" and "f" are the same letter in Hebrew). Therefore, a number of commentators have suggested that "atonement" means "covering," just as Noah covered the Ark with pitch. From this some have suggested that animal sacrifices merely covered over sins with blood, so that God (symbolically) would not see them until the time when Messiah's blood would take sins away.

This understanding has no basis. The meaning of the Hebrew root for atonement (k-p-r) is very different in the Piel verb form (*kiper*) versus the Kal verb form (*kafar*). In the Piel form, which is how it is used on all contexts related to sacrifice, the verb means to "wipe away." You can see how the two meanings are related. In the Kal form, the idea of the verb is wiping something *onto* a surface (to cover it) while in the Piel it means to wipe something *away* from a surface.

Therefore, when we read in Leviticus 16:16, "he shall atone the Holy Place from the impurities of the people of Israel and from their transgressions, even all their sins," the meaning is: he will wipe them away. The idea, which we will expand upon in chapter 4, is that the impurities and also the transgressions of Israel are like pollution which leaves a film of dirt on the Holy Place. The blood wipes away the pollution. It is ritual detergent, to use one of Milgrom's phrases.

From the Impurities of the Children of Israel

The study of impurity (often translated uncleanness) will occupy us in chapter 4. For now, we should note that impurity is a different category than sin. People and things may be pure or impure (clean or unclean). A third category, things and people being holy, is entirely different. To be pure or clean is not necessarily to be holy.

If impurity is not sin, what is it? Why is it such a focus in the Torah? Why do we not hear more about it in theologies of atonement? How does the Torah idea of purity and impurity contribute to our understanding of atonement and even Messiah's death? The answer is: the study of purity laws is crucial for a theology of atonement. There is no proper understanding of atonement without it.

From the Transgressions of the Children of Israel

The second thing that the Yom Kippur ritual cleansed away from the Holy Place is transgression, synonymous in verse 16 with sin. The Holy Place is the innermost room of the Temple, in which we find the Ark of the Covenant and its golden cover with the statues of the cherubim. God's Presence or Glory dwells in here. And in this place, God does not desire any pollution from Israel's impurity and/or transgression. The place of God's Glory is to be kept clean from both.

The commandments of the Torah contain clues to what transgression means to God. Not every transgression is spelled out in Torah. Much of Torah's teaching on what is good and what is evil comes in categories and by broad commands such as "love your neighbor" and "justice, justice you shall pursue." A thorough study of the qualities and actions God loves versus the ones he hates is a lifetime pursuit (not the work of a few hours of reading). The idea of a world without these transgressions is very much implied by the Torah and the Temple regulations. Such a transgression-free world is more than hinted at in the Yom Kippur ritual. But how will God bring this about? Torah does not say.

The Scapegoat in Leviticus 16

In the Babylonian purging ritual for the key temples of the city, a ram's decapitated body was thrown in the river and its head sent into the desert. In Israel's purging ritual the high priest leaned both hands (not the usual one hand from the sacrificial procedure) on the goat and confessed Israel's transgressions over it. It was then sent to an "uninhabitable place" (verse 22), where it was sent to Azazel (probably the name of a goat demon; verses 8, 10, 26).

What is the difference between what this live goat ritual

accomplished, and the blood ritual in the Holy Place and on the Tent? The blood ritual atoned (purged) the Holy Place and the Tent from the pollution caused by un-purified impurities and un-repented and un-sacrificed-for sins. That is, when Israelites did not follow whichever procedure was commanded to purify them, their impurity traveled like air pollution (see chapter 4). And the sins for which people never bothered to bring an offering during the year, these spread a cloud of contamination also which defiled God's Holy Place and the Tent. The blood of the sacrificed goat was like ritual detergent to clean away the besmirching of God's dwelling place.

But the live goat did something else. The collective guilt (Hebrew, *avon*) of the people—not their feelings of shame, but the actual guilt they bore which would result in divine wrath—was placed symbolically on the goat and removed from their collective place. Guilt was sent away.

Limitations, Ideals, and Yom Kippur

But the Yom Kippur or Day of Purgation rituals, as much as they suggest defilement being cleansed and guilt being sent away, are incomplete. They imply an ideal that is never achieved. The more we understand impurity, the Divine Presence, transgression, and guilt, the more we realize the priestly laws imply an ideal. The ideal is a death-less, sin-less community.

But the atoning of the Holy Place and Tent leave the people unchanged. The forgiveness offered for the pollution caused by the people does not result in those people being forever changed. The sending away of guilt on a live goat affects no change either.

The guilt leaves and comes right back. The contamination is cleansed, but immediately starts building up again. Death is symbolically despised and yet death occurs continually. Where is the realization of Yom Kippur? When will it be? How will God bring it about? Or is an unachievable ideal not truly promised?

Our quest to understand atonement needs more information. Before delving more deeply into the meaning of impurities, it is necessary to establish the meaning of another theme in Torah: the Glory which dwelt in the Holy Place and in various forms appeared to people. The Divine Presence in the inner room of the Temple is the heart of Torah's theology. The Divine Presence is also the heart of Messiah's identity. Torah and Messiah converge on the idea of the Divine One who dwells with us.

Chapter 3
The Divine Glory over the Cherubim

I call them mystery-blockers. They are unspoken assumptions about the nature of God, faith, and knowledge that cause readers to overlook the mystical themes that are present all through the Bible. Mystery is the perception that there is much beyond our knowing, that what we can perceive is only a fraction of something much greater. Mystery-blockers are naive reductions of sublime reality to knowable substitutes. The first one is the simplistic and anthropomorphic view of God. He is the "great, old man on the throne."

In this misreading, people see the texts in Genesis, for example, in very non-mystical ways. Forgive what could be considered blasphemous and let me sadly read for you a mental translation of what many people are seeing when they read Genesis:

> In the beginning, the Old Man in heaven created the heav-
> ens and the earth . . . Now the White-Bearded One said,
> "Let there be light and there was light."

The God of Israel is not Zeus. Anthropomorphic descriptions of him are carefully balanced by a continual reminder that he is beyond knowing fully; his paths beyond searching out. Jewish mystics say God is the *Ein Sof* (the Without End). A famous anonymous Christian mystic says he "dwells in a cloud of unknowing."

The opposite mystery-blocker is the rationalist view of God, as being completely beyond the range of human experience (transcendent) and uninvolved personally in the world, history, and human experience. The God of Deism is perfectly transcendent, the great clockmaker in the sky who wound up creation like a clock and has not been back to visit. We are only the merest minuscule microscopic organisms on a grain of sand far from his concern.

The God revealed to Israel, and in Yeshua, is not the philosopher's God. The chief difference is that the God of the Bible is living, present. Philosophy makes rational inquiry absolute. Prophets make experience of the divine absolute. Reason alone does not explain life. To reason has been added revelation (God's revealing of himself; divine disclosure).

And as we seek to know God, to understand his ways and what atonement means, we must consider this verse and what it tells us:

> *And let them make Me a sanctuary that I may dwell among*
> *them (Exodus 25:8, JPS).*

The Tabernacle as Incarnation

God is very involved in the world, in human experience, in history. Yet God is also transcendent (above everything), omnipresent (everything is in his presence), and without end. This leads to a puzzle: how can the Infinite enter finite space? How can the One for whom all things are in his Presence be present in a place?

The ancient rabbis thought about these things. In one parable, we read:

> *It may be likened to a cave situated by the seashore. The*
> *sea rages and the cave is filled with water, but the sea is*
> *not diminished. Similarly, the Tent of Meeting was filled*
> *with the radiance of the Shekhinah, which was not diminished in the universe.*
> *(Numbers Rabbah, XII.4, Soncino Edition).*

And so Moses, on the mountain receiving instruction from

God, was told, "Let them make me a sanctuary." A sanctuary is a "holy place," which in ancient times meant a shrine with an inner room. God said he would show Moses a pattern according to which he was to have it built. And, most importantly, that God wanted it built so he could "tent among them." The word usually rendered "dwell" is *shakhan* (the root word for *mishkhan*/ Tabernacle and also for *Shekhinah*/Presence). In *The JPS Torah Commentary* on Exodus, Nahum Sarna says, "The verb conveys the idea of a temporary lodging in a tent and characterizes the nomadic style of life."

God wants to tent among the Israelites. He will leave the heavens and dwell in a place on earth. But no one imagined that this meant God would dwell only in the sanctuary. While dwelling in the Tabernacle and later the Temple that replaced it, he nonetheless appears in many other places and he never ceases to be the Omnipresent.

The sanctuary of Israel is a kind of incarnation. In Yeshua, God was here dwelling as a man (the divine Messiah). In Israel's sanctuary, God was within the people as a whole, filling the nation so that any who looked on them would say, "God is with them." Israel is the body and the Glory of God is the infilling (more will be said about this in chapter 8, "The Divine Glory Incarnate").

Paul refers to something like this in Romans 9:4. The Yeshua-followers in Rome are confused about the Jewish community there. It seems as if Messiah is not with the Jews of Rome. They wonder if the Jews have been replaced and some have already suggested it. But Paul says, "They are Israelites, and to them belong the adoption, the glory, the covenants, the giving of the law, the worship, and the promises" (Romans 9:4, ESV). The word "glory" in Romans 9:4 ought to be capitalized, as it refers to the Presence in the Jerusalem Temple of Paul's day.

Isaiah calls Israel the servant and God's witness, a light to the gentiles (41:8; 42:19; 43:10; 44:1-2, 21, 26; 45:4; 48:20). Exodus calls Israel the priestly people, a holy nation, chosen from among all peoples for a special role (19:5-6). What makes Israel special is that they are the bearers of the divine Presence. The concentration of this Presence is the sanctuary—Tabernacle—Temple in the midst of Israel. The exact center of this dwelling is above the Ark, over the atoning place (traditionally the "mercy seat") inside the sanctuary.

The Presence, the Ark, and the Atoning Place (Mercy Seat)

God wants to dwell with people. In the exact place where he dwells, there is an atoning place. The dwelling of God with humanity is combined with the idea of atonement.

When Israel first built the sanctuary which God revealed to Moses in Exodus 25, it was a tent that they could set up, take down, and bring with them in their wilderness wanderings. This tent was called the Tabernacle (*mishkan*). Then it wandered with them from place to place in Israel during the days of the judges. Then David brought it to (or made a new one in) Jerusalem. Then Solomon replaced it with a Temple (and some say he originally set up the Tabernacle inside the Temple).

The one constant in this changing location of the sanctuary of the Lord is the Ark. It is a fairly small box of acacia wood overlaid with gold about four and half feet long, and just over two feet wide and high (Exodus 25:10).

On its top is a cover, traditionally called the "mercy seat" in many English translations. It is the "atoning place" (*kapporet*). On this "atoning place" covered with gold atop the Ark, are two golden cherubim (angelic beings, part animal and part human, like sphinxes) with their wings spread toward each other.

The atonement or purging of Israel's impurity and wrongdoing happen here (see chapter 2, "Day of Purgation"). This is the place on which the high priest dashes blood for purgation, once a year (at Yom Kippur, the Day of Purgation/Atonement) and in times of ritual emergency. Interestingly, and few translations make this apparent, Paul calls Yeshua the "atoning place" (Greek *hilastairion*, which is a translation of the Hebrew *kapporet*) in Romans 3:25. The connections between Torah and Messiah abound.

And the atoning place is also related to the Presence of the Lord. How so? More than once we read in the Bible, "The Lord, who is enthroned above the cherubim" (1 Samuel 4:4; 2 Samuel 6:2; 2 Kings 19:15; 1 Chronicles 13:6; Psalms 80:1; 99:1; Isaiah 37:16). What exactly does the Ark correspond to? Why is an Ark with a cover topped by golden cherubim-sphinxes the fitting place for atonement? The link between God's Presence and atonement will become clearer and clearer.

Cherub-Sphinxes and the Glory

Not only do we have many verses describing the Presence of the Lord as "enthroned above the cherubim," but also in Leviticus 16:2, God said: "I will appear in the cloud over the atoning place (mercy seat)." Atop this golden Ark cover are two cherubim. We read about cherubim in a few places in the Bible, including the story of Adam and Eve's expulsion from the Garden. Two cherubim with flaming swords guarded the way back (Genesis 3:24).

The Mesopotamians and Egyptians also had cherubim (*kuribu* in the Assyrian language corresponds to *kheruv* in Hebrew and "cherub" in English). They are sphinxes, part animal and part human, such as a lion with eagle's wings and a human head.

One clue to the possible appearance of the cherubim on God's Ark is in Ezekiel 1:5–11. When the prophet saw a vision of God's chariot-throne, he gave us a description of the "living beings" who bore the Lord. It is possible that his description is what the cherubim in the sanctuary on the Ark cover (atoning place, mercy seat) looked like. They had the body of a bull, wings like an eagle, human hands under the wings, and a four-sided face (human, lion, bull, eagle). Perhaps the cherubim in the sanctuary were not this elaborate or perhaps they were.

What are sphinxes doing in the Bible? Perhaps the reality of angelic beings is that they may appear to be whatever form they desire. A consistent pattern in God's manner of revealing himself is that he uses forms and cultural elements familiar to the people. If sphinxes were semi-divine beings in Near Eastern thought, the Bible is telling us there are no gods but only servants of God, heavenly messengers and throne-bearers who serve him. What the peoples around Israel worship are merely the forces of nature and vague notions of beings who, in truth, are God's messengers.

Furthermore, when we understand what exactly the Ark represented in the Near Eastern culture, it will be all the more obvious to us that the cherubim atop the Ark were part of the symbolism. Reality is that there is One with power in heaven, greater than which nothing exists, and that the lesser powers which man is tempted to worship are not deities. In reality the Ark is God's footstool and above the Ark is the invisible throne.

The Footstool and the Throne

In his commentary on Numbers, Jacob Milgrom says, "Israel's religion . . . was imageless from the outset" and they "regarded the Ark not as a representation of the Deity, but only as his footstool" (373–374). In Exodus 20:4 and 19–20 (22–23 in Christian Bibles) we read that the Israelites were not to make images of God nor of lesser "gods" to be companions of God (in pagan worship, gods could have wives, concubines, and companion deities). No representation of God himself was to be made. The Israelites saw that God spoke with them directly from the heavens, that there was no idol. Therefore they were not to make an idol representing God.

Imageless worship was, as far as we know, unheard of. The laws of Exodus 20 are set in opposition to the normal Near Eastern way of doing things. Though there are numerous similarities between the way God is worshipped in Israel and in the nations, the crux passages involve the differences. The nations had sphinxes and sanctuaries, but they did not have the Invisible God who forbade images. Why did he forbid images? In keeping with the consistent tension in scripture between God as Present and yet Omnipresent, above all things and yet dwelling amongst his people, the forbidding of images is so no one can imagine that there is a limit on God's Being and power.

What does it mean that God is "enthroned above the cherubim" (1 Samuel 4:4; 2 Samuel 6:2; 2 Kings 19:15; 1 Chronicles 13:6; Psalms 80:1; 99:1; Isa 37:16)? To understand this description it is helpful to know of pictures left to us from Near Eastern writings, pictures of kings sitting on high thrones with their feet resting on footstools. The footstool was necessary because of the height of the thrones. The kings sat on high thrones to show themselves as exalted over those who attended their court.

Therefore, the Ark is a footstool for God. But where is his throne? It is invisible and is over the Ark, over the atoning place (mercy seat) with its cherubim. As Psalm 99:5 says, "Exalt the Lord our God; worship at his footstool!" Also Psalm 132:5, "Let us go to his dwelling place; let us worship at his footstool!" And if these are not convincing enough to make the connection, we have 1 Chronicles 28:2:

> Then King David rose to his feet and said: "Hear me, my brothers and my people. I had it in my heart to build a house of rest for the ark of the covenant of the Lord and for the footstool of our God, and I made preparations for building (1 Chronicles 28:2, ESV).

The Link Between Heaven and Earth

What does atonement have to do with the Presence of the Omnipresent in the sanctuary (Tabernacle/Temple) of Israel? Everything.

The English word "atonement" is thought to have been coined as a reference to being at one with God (at-one-ment). Although the meaning of the Hebrew word translated as atone and atonement does not in itself mean "being at one with God," this concept does exist in the theology of atonement in Leviticus, the rest of Torah, and the whole Jewish Bible and New Testament.

The place where atonement happens is in the sanctuary, first the Tabernacle (moveable tent) and later the Temple. Of this sanctuary, God said, "let them make Me a sanctuary that I may dwell among them" (Exodus 25:8, JPS).

The specific place where atonement happens is on the Ark cover, once a year at Yom Kippur or in emergencies of impurity, with the rite of Purgation (see chapter 2). This cover is the "atoning place" (usually rendered mercy seat or cover). God says, "I will appear in the cloud over the mercy seat" (Leviticus 16:2, ESV).

The atoning place on the Ark is the link between heaven and earth. But there is a danger in God, the Omnipresent, making a manifestation of his Presence dwell near the people. The danger is that God abhors two things in particular that characterize the human condition (more on what these two things are later). Thus he promises if the people obey, "I will make my dwelling among you, and my soul shall not abhor you" (Leviticus 26:11, ESV).

What does God abhor about his people? Two clues, not as commonly known as they should be, are found in key sections on the laws of purification in the Torah:

> You shall put the Israelites on guard against their uncleanness, lest they die through their uncleanness by defiling My Tabernacle which is among them (Leviticus 15:31, JPS).

> If anyone who has become unclean fails to cleanse himself, that person shall be cut off from the congregation, for he has defiled the Lord's sanctuary. The water of lustration was not dashed on him: he is unclean (Numbers 19:20, JPS).

The danger of being near to God's Presence is death. The fatal thing about us that will cause death is uncleanness (impurity). Impurity defiles (pollutes). The solution is to constantly "cleanse" impurity (purify it). Atonement, then, is about being near God and dwelling with him. It is about our ability to survive near his Presence.

Leviticus 26:11–12 imply that if the people do not obey, his Presence will depart. God says "my soul will abhor you" (Leviticus 26:30) and "the land will vomit you out" (Leviticus 18:28). In Ezekiel, the prophet who explores priestly themes more than any other, we read that this is, in fact, what happened to Jerusalem preceding 586 BCE (when the Babylonians destroyed it). In Ezekiel 10 the Presence (the Glory) departed in stages from the threshold of the "house" (Temple) and over the Eastern Gate.

Atonement involves the Presence of God with us. And to understand more about it, we have to learn what impurity (uncleanness) meant in the Torah. It is a system designed by God to teach Israel what he abhors and why atonement is necessary.

Chapter 4
Ritual Pollution: Sin and Death

Some people think the laws of uncleanness (impurity) in Torah have to do with the idea of a "cultural taboo." The word for "uncleanness" is *tum'ah*, as in "If any one of all your offspring throughout your generations approaches the holy things . . . while he has a *tum'ah* [an uncleanness], that person shall be cut off from my presence" (Leviticus 22:3, ESV). What is an uncleanness, an impurity? Does it mean "dirty"? Is it symbolic dirt? Is it like the idea of a "cultural taboo"?

Say you are at a shopping mall. You have a half-finished beverage in a cup with a lid and straw. You are by yourself and urgently need to go to the restroom. Do you bring your cup in with you? If you leave it on the table in the food court, a worker may dispose of it. But do you bring it inside to a place where there may be bad smells and filth? Is the unsanitary nature of a public restroom like a miasma of air pollution which will certainly enter your cup and "pollute" your beverage if you bring it inside? What if you bring your beverage only as far as the sinks where people wash their hands? Is that acceptable? If you do bring your drink inside, will people look at you with momentary disgust? Is your concern really about hygiene and safety from bacterial infections or is it really the cultural taboo that matters to you?

"Unclean," says the leper, her mouth covered as she passes, "unclean" (see Leviticus 13:45–46). Is the leper dirty? Is biblical leprosy contagious by touch? Actually, no.

Or in another scenario, you are an ancient Israelite picking up your garment from the floor in the morning. You find a dead mouse on it, touching the fabric. Now you may not wear it, but must immerse it in water and wait until after sundown before the garment is "clean" again (Leviticus 11:29–38). Even if you could wash it thoroughly and dry it over a cooking fire before dinner, you still may not wear it. Is your garment contaminated?

Welcome to the strange world of the purity laws of Torah. They get stranger upon close investigation. When I first encountered them during my college years when I began to read the Bible, I decided they were arbitrary. I may have read that in a commentary (if so, an uninformed one). It was as if God, the maker of arcane rules and the authority figure who must be obeyed, had declared, "Wearing purple is a sin; whoever does it will be cut off."

It was one more reason for me to suspect that God gave a bad Law from which Christ came to set us free. I wasn't sure the reason God—the loving God, or so people told me—would do something like that. Maybe he wanted people to live under a burdensome system for a long time so that when freedom came in Messiah, they would praise him and believe all the more. Naturally, even then, I thought that was a weak notion of God and the Torah. But it fit well with things I heard at the church I was attending. "Those things were nailed to the cross," people would tell me.

The Puzzling List of Impure Conditions and Actions

In Leviticus 10:10 (JPS), as God instructs Aaron, and through him all of the priests, he says, "you must distinguish between the sacred and the profane, and between the unclean and the clean." The priests are to teach the people all of God's statutes, especially the laws of purity and purification. All things are either sacred (holy) or profane (common) and what is profane may be either pure (clean) or impure (unclean).

This can be represented graphically as follows:

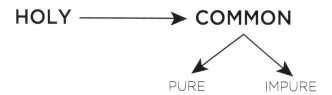

That which is holy has been designated for some divine purpose and must not be defiled by contact with the impure, (more on this later) and that which is impure must be purified so that the pollution does not remain. What conditions and actions are impure?

» *Touching the carcass of an unclean animal, Leviticus 11:24–28.*

» *Vessels and objects on which dead, unclean animals have fallen, Leviticus 11:29–38.*

» *A woman after childbirth, Leviticus 12.*

» *A person judged to have scale disease (biblical "leprosy"), Leviticus 13:1–3.*

» *Anyone who has contact with a scale-diseased person (not stated, but implied).*

» *A man with gonorrhea (see Milgrom for evidence), Leviticus 15:2–3.*

» *Anyone who touches a man with gonorrhea or what he sat on, Leviticus 15:4–11.*

» *A man with an emission of semen of any kind, Leviticus 15:16–17.*

» *A woman and man after intercourse, Leviticus 15:18.*

» *A menstruating woman or anyone who touches what she sat on, Leviticus 15:19–23.*

» *Anyone who has touched a human corpse, Numbers 19:11–13.*

» *Anyone contracting corpse uncleanness indirectly, Numbers 19:14–19.*

The Durations and Purification Procedures for Impurity

Leviticus 15:31 is a crucial verse for understanding the purity laws of Torah: "Thus you shall keep the people of Israel separate

from their uncleanness, lest they die in their uncleanness by defiling my tabernacle that is in their midst" (ESV). We can infer
from this verse that it is no crime against God or other people
to become impure. But it is a transgression if a person does not
follow the procedures for purification. These laws and procedures
do not apply today without the existence of the Temple in Jerusalem, since being "clean" or "unclean" only relates to entering the
Temple courts and participating in certain rituals near the divine
Presence.

What must a person do to purify themselves or objects that
have become unclean? Some of them are quite involved and all
of them interrupt the course of life and require attention. These
are based on tables in Milgrom's commentary on Leviticus 1–16
and are given in descending order of duration and severity (986–
999):

» *Scale-diseased person (a.k.a. leper)—duration of sick-
ness plus seven days, shaving, sprinkling, laundering,
bathing, second shaving, laundering, and bathing, plus
multiple sacrifices and daubing with blood twice.*

» *Woman after childbirth—forty one or eighty one days
impure total, laundering and bathing, sacrifices.*

» *Person with genital discharge (gonorrhea)—duration
plus seven days, laundering and bathing, sacrifices.*

» *Corpse-contaminated priest (a priest who touched a
dead person)—fourteen days, sprinkling twice, laundering and bathing, sacrifices.*

» *Corpse-contaminated Nazirite (a Nazirite who touched
a dead person)—seven days, sprinkling twice, shaving,
laundering and bathing, multiple sacrifices.*

» *A person who accidentally neglects purification (Leviticus 5:1–13)—duration plus one day, bathing, sacrifice plus grain offering.*

» *Corpse-contaminated lay-person (an Israelite who
touched a dead person)—seven days, sprinkling twice,*

laundering and bathing.

» *Menstruate—seven days, laundering and bathing.*

» *Handler of red heifer, scapegoat, or sin offering—one day, laundering and bathing.*

» *Man after semen is emitted (after sexual intercourse or any other ejaculation)—one day, laundering and bathing.*

» *Person after touching carcass of unclean animal—one day, laundering and bathing.*

» *Person secondarily contaminated (by touching someone impure) (Leviticus 15; 22:4-7; Numbers 19)—one day, laundering and bathing.*

Christianity, Judaism, and Purification

Among the procedures to purify a person or object, one stands out in terms of the later history of Judaism: immersion in water. In many cases, purification requires clothing to be laundered (immersed in water). In every case, bathing in water is required.

In Judaism, this is the ritual bath. The bath itself is called a *mikvah* and is often housed in a building near a synagogue, in modern times. The process of ritual bathing is called *t'villah* (immersion) and is still commonly practiced by women monthly for ceremonial (ritual) purification from the impurity of menstruation. Men attend the *mikvah* especially before the High Holidays in the fall. Prior to Passover, dishes and vessels are often immersed in a small *mikvah* designed for vessels and not persons.

In Christianity, this is baptism. The Jewish ritual bath was used frequently in some places, such as at the Temple where visitors to the inner courts had to be immersed and among some Essenes who immersed themselves twice daily. Yet, in the New Testament, John the Baptizer practiced a special form of immersion, which was likely a one-time event and which we should assume he did not mean to replace the practice of ritual bathing according to the Torah. This special baptism was like ritual bathing, but it was also different.

Normal ritual bathing in the Baptizer's day was in pools (though bodies of water were also permitted). John's baptism was in the free-flowing water of the Jordan, which was also significant as the place by which Israel first entered the land. John's baptism was a sort of re-start, a repentance marked with a ritual bath and to be followed up by a dedicated life.

Yeshua himself was baptized in this way and either he or his disciples continued the work of John for a time. Just before his ascension, Yeshua commanded that his disciples use baptism as the entrance ceremony for new disciples. Christian baptism in our time comes from the ritual bathing of Leviticus.

Yet in Leviticus there was no bathing for repentance from sin. This was an innovation of John the Baptizer. Nonetheless, as we come to understand more about what impurity is and what affect it has, the baptism rite of Christianity will make even more sense.

The Meaning of Impurity

By now it should be clear that the purity laws of Torah are unusual, that it is a sin not to follow the purification procedures, that the priests would learn and teach the details of this system to laypeople in Israel, and that God is either an arbitrary dictator, or the causes of impurity have an important symbolic meaning.

In the explanation of their meaning which Jacob Milgrom proposed in his commentary on Leviticus 1–16, and which has found wide acceptance, there is a partial rejection of many other theories. Scholars have proposed various theories for what the causes of impurity might have in common: sin, aesthetics, fear of demons, holiness of the sanctuary, separation of Israel, health, magic, arbitrary priestly power. Yet none of them, in my opinion, explains all of the types of impurity as well as the theory of Jacob Milgrom. Having said this, we do not deny that the system made more sense in the culture of the time. Their aesthetics and ideas about impurity from the larger culture played a role in God's teaching. If Torah had not been given in the early days of Israel, but instead, it was given in our time, no doubt the list of impure conditions and actions would be slightly different.

Yet once the rationale of the purity laws is explained, it seems as if it should have been evident all along. Though the purity laws may seem arcane in our time, we would have to guess that these practices were, in their culture, as natural for them as us choosing not to take a soft drink into a public restroom.

Milgrom explains the impurities simply:

> *The bodily impurities enumerated in [Torah] . . . focus on*
> *four phenomena: death, blood, semen, and scale disease.*
> *Their common denominator is death (1,002).*

Loss of blood or semen is loss of life. Scale disease makes a person look like a corpse and is a form of rot or spreading death. Even the dietary restrictions of Leviticus 11 can be explained as limiting death to certain species (that is, if Israelites can only eat certain animals, they won't kill as many animals).

The message of God's purity laws is simple: he is the God of life, not death. This theology has its roots in Genesis, where God declares the death penalty for human wrongdoing and disloyalty. Evil is man's choice, not God's. Thus, death is not part of the perfect world God intended and which he will one day bring to completion.

Milgrom adds a twist: whereas other cultures feared demons and magic, God taught Israel a different theology of sacrifice and worship. The battle is not between demonic forces and human, but between life and death. Death was set loose by man's rebellion against God's commandment (1,003). The cause of suffering is not random, malevolent, invisible forces (demons) nor is it the caprice of immature deities (polytheism).

Suffering is less than God's ideal, but in the present time it must be endured. Death is a reality of human life. Yet the laws of clean and unclean reveal something: God does not want human death, real or symbolic, near his Temple. We may regard this as a hint that something better will one day exist. And the separation of death from the holy place where the Presence dwells is central to Torah.

Mouldering Self-Portraits

I've never read *The Picture of Dorian Gray* by Oscar Wilde. But I am familiar with the image created by Wilde in this novel; a gruesome image of the reality of evil. Dorian Gray had a portrait of himself commissioned. He engaged in a life of unrestrained pleasures and his own physical beauty became of utmost importance to his happiness. He made a pact, apparently with the devil, stating that he would not age, but only his portrait would.

The portrait, hidden away in the Gray estate, grew more hideous with each passing year while Gray himself remained youthful and beautiful.

In the one-volume commentary on Leviticus Milgrom wrote:

> *Like this Wilde character, the priestly writers would claim that sin may not blotch the face of the sinner, but it is certain to blotch the face of the sanctuary, and, unless quickly expunged, God's presence will depart (Milgrom 2004, 32).*

Thus we read in Numbers 19:20 (JPS), the chapter on human corpses, the ashes of the red heifer, and impurity from any contact with a corpse or even coming under the roof with one: "If anyone who has become unclean fails to cleanse himself, that person shall be cut off from the congregation, for he has defiled the Lord's sanctuary. The water of lustration was not dashed on him: he is unclean."

To defile something, in the context of ritual laws, means to bring impurity into contact with things that are holy. The sanctuary (Tabernacle/Temple) is holy. It is designated for God's purpose. Defiling holy things can cause death as Nadab and Abihu discovered (Leviticus 10:1–2), as did some Philistines who took the Ark (1 Samuel 5), some Israelites who looked at the uncovered Ark (1 Samuel 6:19–21), and Uzzah who touched the Ark (2 Samuel 6:7).

Any signs of Dorian Gray's aging and drawing nearer to death traveled through the air into the hidden room where he kept his portrait. He appeared to be well. Likewise, in Torah, defilement (pollution) traveled from all over the land of Israel to the Temple when Israelites failed to cleanse impurity (Leviticus 15:31; Numbers 19:20). The wrongdoing of the people had to be purified also, but that required sacrifices and blood (see chapters 6–8).

The people of Israel may have appeared to be fine and well, but the reality of their stains of death and wrongdoing were invisible pollution on the Temple. Water and blood cleansed this impurity. And the system God taught his people, which affected so many aspects of daily life, implied a promise of something better. It implied that in the ideal world, death and evil have no place. Could the ritual purification laws even imply life from the dead?

Other Purification Rites and Resurrection

Besides bathing and laundering (baptizing), the purification laws of Torah have other elements as well. In some cases a person had to shave, an act which is related to the bathing and laundering. In all cases a person had to wait for a designated period, sometimes merely until sundown. Perhaps the waiting suggests that in the course of time, God will make all things clean.

Yet two other very unusual rites of purification deserve

comment. One of them will first require an understanding of the sacrificial system. The priests were to find a red heifer (cow) and to take it outside of the courts of the sanctuary (eventually the Mount of Olives became the place for this), slaughter it in that place, sprinkle some of its blood seven times in the direction of the sanctuary, and then burn it whole (blood and all), along with hyssop, scarlet yarn, and cedar wood. We should note here that hyssop was used to dash blood, and was associated with blood sacrifice, and also that scarlet yarn and cedar wood are both red (the general color of blood). These ashes of the red heifer were placed in tiny quantities of water which was then dashed against the person who was contaminated by corpse impurity (Numbers 19:1–19).

Some aspects of the red heifer rite require an understanding of sin offerings (see chapter 8). Yet we should note here that this ritual of dashing water mingled with ashes of the red heifer is a possible background to Paul's puzzling statement in 1 Corinthians 15:29 about people "being baptized on behalf of their dead" (ESV). Remember that the Greek word "baptize" in the New Testament relates to the Jewish practice of ceremonial washing. Remember that the person being dashed with water became impure "on behalf of their dead," which is to say, they cared for the corpse (carried it, touched it) of their loved one.

Yet the startling thing is Paul's suggestion that the ritual washing on behalf of the dead (from Numbers 19, if that is what he is referring to) implies resurrection or life after death. How did Paul reach this conclusion? It could just be that Paul was an astute Torah scholar (and Pharisee).

The one remaining ritual purification procedure brings us even closer to this point: if the water with ashes from the red heifer pointed toward life from the dead, all the more so the purification ceremony for a "leper" (scale-diseased person). Once the scale-diseased person was declared clean, and after a wait of seven days, the priest was to perform a ritual with two birds, hyssop, cedar wood, scarlet yarn, and an earthenware vessel with pure water. One bird he killed so that its blood fell in the water.

The other bird he held with the hyssop, cedar, and scarlet in his hand. He then would dip these into the water and sprinkle the cleansed person seven times. Afterward he would release the live bird (Leviticus 14:1–7).

How shall we understand this? The scale-diseased person was regarded as the walking dead. His or her appearance was like a mold-covered corpse (white and blemished). He or she was required to cover the mouth and say, "Unclean" (Leviticus 13:45–46). Compare this to Lamentations 4:14–15, which describes the survivors of the destruction of Jerusalem in 586 BCE. They had been in contact with so much death, they walked the streets "defiled with blood" and cried to all who came near "Away! Unclean!" (JPS). This is an extreme rite of mourning and the scale-diseased person walked daily in mourning for their own death (Milgrom, 804-805).

The bird killed over the water represents the scale-diseased person's life before becoming pure again. The bird released represents their new life from the dead. The ultimate end of ritual purification is the complete elimination of death. The ritual purification procedures strongly hint at this. Yeshua himself saw that in Torah there is a thread of resurrection: "He is not the God of the dead but the God of the living!" (Matthew 22:32, DHE). All the purity laws tell us that God remains separate from death and will not have it brought into his holy place. His people must continually cleanse the presence of any death in the land. It may be that, though he has not communicated to Israel a plan, God has in mind the death of death and restoration of life to all of his people.

Chapter 5

Hebrews Knows Its Stuff

Somewhere I read that the book of Hebrews was a bungled attempt at using the Torah's words about the sanctuary and priesthood to become a cheap allegory about Jesus. I no longer remember what article or book I was reading. But I filed that away for future thought. Does Hebrews know its stuff?

It is true that the "creative" ways Hebrews uses verses from the Hebrew Bible is troubling for modern readers. Most of us are attuned to the idea of plain meaning, of interpreting writings by their context. But in Hebrews there are some unusual readings of scripture. How do we account for this? This is important in a book on atonement and Yeshua, because Hebrews, more than any other book in the Bible, brings together atonement in Torah with atonement in Messiah. If Hebrews is a cheap allegory, well, needless to say that would be disappointing.

To understand Hebrews, it is helpful to be a reader of books of the same genre as Hebrews. What genre is that? Midrash, an early rabbinical style of writing from the land of Israel (which will be explained as this chapter progresses). Günther Zuntz, in an important book on the text of the New Testament, said this about Hebrews in 1946: "It is a midrash in rhetorical Greek prose—it is a homily" (Bruce, 25).

What is a homily? What is a midrash? How do these categories relate to Hebrews? Isn't Hebrews a letter?

First, a homily is a kind of sermon, but more specifically it is a comment on a specific text or set of texts meant to make them applicable and memorable. How do we guess that Hebrews is a homily? Start with Hebrews 13:22, in which the unknown author calls it a "word of exhortation." Compare this to Acts 13:15, when the synagogue in Pisidian Antioch asked if Paul the Pharisee had a "word of exhortation" to share after the Torah and prophets readings (Bruce, 25). They wanted to know if Paul would give a homily (referred to in modern synagogues as a *d'rash*, related to the word midrash).

Second, a midrash is a peculiarly Jewish kind of homily. Midrashic writings cite texts from the Hebrew Bible and use them in creative ways. We have many midrashic homilies preserved in rabbinic literature, from the rabbinic movement in Israel (the Babylonian community did not favor this kind of midrash), written down starting in the second century. We also see examples of midrashic ways of using scripture creatively in Yeshua's teaching and in Paul's. And Hebrews definitely does use strings of Hebrew Bible verses in creative ways!

Third, note that Hebrews uses the Greek version of the Bible (not the Hebrew) and uses some specific Greek rhetorical forms. One that stands out is called *synkrisis*, which means praising a particular individual by comparing them to similar individuals or groups and asserting their superiority. Hebrews does that again and again, comparing Yeshua to angels, the priesthood, Melchizedek, Moses, etc., and asserting his superiority. There is nothing unusual about a Jewish writer of the period using the Greek Bible and Greek methods. Judaism in that period was heavily influenced by Greek language and ideas.

So, we have in the book of Hebrews a learned writer, using a more refined literary Greek than most of the New Testament. He (or she) knows the Greek Bible (and likely the Hebrew Bible as well, as there are indications he is quite familiar with midrashic uses of scripture). He (or she) knows his (or her) stuff (Priscilla is a potential candidate among many for authorship). And his (her) writing is a homily well within the sphere of rabbinic midrash. It is not allegory.

Not Allegory but Midrash

Not long before the unknown author of Hebrews, there was Philo of Alexandria. To a modern reader, unfamiliar with differences between allegory and midrashic interpretation, there might appear to be great similarity between the way Philo uses scripture and Hebrews. Consider how the two almost-contemporary writers use the Melchizedek story (Genesis 14). They both seem to play fast and loose with the plain meaning. But are they really that similar in method?

In Philo's allegory on Melchizedek in *Legum Allegoriae 3:82*, Melchizedek becomes a symbol for reason (Bruce, 28). Philo says, in reference to Genesis 14:18: "For reason is a priest . . . entertaining lofty and sublime and magnificent ideas about him, 'for he is the priest of the Most High God'" (translation by C.D. Yonge, *The Works of Philo*, Hendrickson).

Hebrews doesn't do allegory. Some prefer to call the literary method of Hebrews typology. A typology is a literary foreshadowing of a person or thing from the past, signifying someone or something else who will come later. Yet when examined closely, Hebrews uses midrashic proofs to connect Melchizedek with Yeshua. The connection is, perhaps, tighter than the word typology would suggest.

Consider Hebrews 7:1–10 on Melchizedek. Not understanding the creativity of midrash, and assuming that somehow Hebrews is doing a plain reading of Genesis 14, many interpret this passage literally. Compare in this following two lists a literal understanding of Hebrews 7:1–10 and a midrashic understanding:

A Literal Reading of Hebrews 7:1–10

» *Melchizedek is the "king of righteousness" and "king of peace."*

» *He is literally Yeshua appearing before the incarnation.*

» *He is not a historical person.*

» *He has no father or mother (since he is the Son of God appearing prior to Yeshua's birth via Mary).*

» *Melchizedek is pre-existent and eternal.*

» *Abraham tithed to Melchizedek because he under-*

stood him to be divine.

» *Melchizedek is more important in God's plan than Abraham.*

A Midrashic Reading of Hebrews 7:1–10

» *Melchizedek's name and title are a foreshadowing of Messiah.*

» *He is a historical person, but the account of him stands out as an anomaly in Genesis, leading to a sense that he is a mysterious foreshadowing.*

» *In Genesis his character is a rare exception, having no genealogy as all other important characters do.*

» *Even his tribe and people are not named.*

» *His birth and death are not recorded, which is unusual for a figure so important in the Genesis story.*

» *Abraham tithed to him because he recognized Melchizedek as serving the true God.*

» *Abraham's tithe can creatively be seen as Levi tithing to Melchizedek.*

» *This is a hint that the kind of priest Melchizedek is precedes the Levitical priesthood and is of greater significance.*

» *Note: King David and Psalm 110 will provide more solid backing for what Hebrews has to say about Melchizedek.*

As F.F. Bruce notes concerning the way Hebrews reads in the Bible: "The Old Testament writings are treated by our author as a *mashal*, a parable or mystery that awaits explanation" (27).

But isn't this a problem? If everyone reads between the

lines, ignores the plain meaning, and finds creative symbolisms all through the Bible, won't it end up meaning anything and everything? If it means anything someone wants it to mean, it ends up meaning nothing.

How Midrash Works in Hebrews

To grasp what Hebrews is doing, it is good to compare it to rabbinic midrashic literature. Most Bible readers are unfamiliar with midrash. In the collection known as Midrash Rabbah, key examples of midrash are Song of Songs Rabbah, Leviticus Rabbah, Lamentations Rabbah, and so on. An older translation in English exists (by Soncino Press) for those who would like to delve into this kind of writing. Yet many will find it hard to understand, because the midrashes are given in shorthand writing. Hebrews is like these midrashic writings, except that it is a full sermon, explaining in more depth how the writer is deriving his (or her) ideas.

Midrash is not random symbolism. Midrash starts with a good and solidly derived point of theology. Song of Songs Rabbah, for example, starts with the idea that Israel is the chosen people, that God gave the Torah for Israel to study, and that until Messiah comes the study and practice of Torah is what Israel should occupy itself with. Hebrews starts with the idea that Yeshua is divine, is to be worshipped, and is our priest who brings us from this present world into the world to come by his work.

This theological basis is what keeps midrash from being "wrong." You can judge the worth of a midrash by the truth of its message, not the literal application of its method. So, you may object to interpreting Melchizedek mysteriously and insist Melchizedek is simply a historical king-priest. The writer of Hebrews would simply say to you, "Of course Melchizedek was a real person." If you further objected, "Then you have no basis to play these symbolic games and make Melchizedek a mystery type of Messiah," the writer of Hebrews would surely respond to defeat you.

The art of midrash is just as objective as the theological foundation of midrash. The writer of Hebrews would take up your challenge, "If there is nothing mysterious about Melchizedek, explain why his character does not follow the narrative rules of Genesis." A skillful midrash is based on some oddity in the text. The sudden appearance of a tribe-less king-priest so honored by Abraham our father lacking genealogy and explanation is an oddity. The fact that his name and titles are so pregnant with meaning is a further oddity. The idea of Abraham tithing to some Canaanite king-priest is equally a mystery. The writer of Hebrews might say, "Don't you think God places riddles in history and in the scriptures?"

If you are still not convinced, the writer of Hebrews could press you further: "How is it that King David acted in some ways as a priest?" If you know your history, you know that only Levites were to be priests, that King Saul got into trouble for doing priestly things instead of waiting for Samuel (1 Samuel 15), and that David put on a linen ephod and danced before the Ark (2 Samuel 6; 1 Chronicles 15). He (or she) would then bring you to Psalm 110.

How could a non-Levite, a king in Israel, justify acting in some kind of priestly role? He would have to do this without violating the restriction of certain priestly activities (handling sacred things, performing sacrificial rites) by Torah to the Levites. So what precedent could he even find for presenting himself as a king-priest?

He could look to the history of the capital city which he founded as the new center of the tribes of Israel: Jerusalem. He could refer back to an earlier king of Salem (Jerusalem) named Melchizedek. He (or a later Davidic king or other writer) could write a Psalm about this kind of kingship. That already would be enough to make Melchizedek a foreshadowing of Messiah. But if that Psalm (Psalm 110) happened also itself to be a hint of a lord greater than King David, the foreshadowing would be even more certain!

Thus, has the writer of Hebrews made a good midrash on Melchizedek, painting him as a shadow of Messiah? Is the midrashic creativity of Hebrews 7:1–10 justified? It certainly is, and the message of Hebrews 7:1–10 for the original audience of Hebrews is clear. Do not abandon your faith in Yeshua. The rejection you may face in the synagogues is hard. But the priesthood of Yeshua was pre-figured before the Levites were ever ordained priests. The priesthood of Yeshua is further-reaching than the Levitical priesthood. The synagogue has the Torah. But in Yeshua you have the Torah plus more—everything Torah was pointing to from the beginning.

The Skillfulness of Hebrews

"I appeal to you, brothers," says the writer, "to bear with my word of exhortation," (13:22, ESV). He (or she) asks how the readers will escape judgment if they neglect such a great salvation from death as is being offered through the way of Yeshua (2:3). The premise of the book is that Yeshua is the highest level of Judaism and Torah. Yet the intended readers are considering renouncing their commitment to the way of Yeshua.

We can guess that synagogue authorities were questioning the strange beliefs of these messianics concerning worshipping Yeshua as one co-equal with God (see James 2:6–7). Some were no longer enthused about the message of Yeshua. Perhaps they were not seeing the heightened level of glory and union with God they expected to see once they started following Yeshua's way. Persecution and bearing reproach for Yeshua are hard (see Hebrews 13:13).

Should these Jewish disciples abandon Yeshua? Can they take comfort in going back to a Yeshua-less Judaism? Or having had a Yeshua-filled Judaism, would they be going backwards by renouncing Yeshua?

The writer of Hebrews has a difficult task. He (or she) must persuade Greek-speaking Jews under intense pressure to bear reproach, to be a counter-cultural movement within Judaism for a messianic heightening of faith and love. To do this well, to be persuasive, the writer will need skill.

So we should prepare ourselves to see certain things in Hebrews:

» *The book uses learned Greek and Hebrew methods.*

» *The use of scripture is similar to the Qumran writings (Dead Sea scrolls) and later rabbinic writings.*

» *The book is based on key texts from the Torah (Bruce cites a theory these came from the Shavuot readings in the triennial Torah lectionary from the time, 26).*

» *The book uses strings of verses to interpret each other and address the need for faith in Yeshua and the necessity of the atonement Yeshua made.*

» *The book regards the Hebrew Bible (Greek translation in particular) as a great parable pointing to present realities.*

» *The book sees in the details of the sanctuary, priestly, and holiness laws, meaning for the present time.*

That is to say, Hebrews brings together Torah and Yeshua like no other book of the New Testament. For our purposes, in a study on Yeshua and atonement, there could hardly be a more important book than Hebrews. Consider the ways the chapters of Hebrews use various kinds of scriptures to address certain problems and issues of faith in Yeshua:

Scripture Lessons In Hebrews

» *Chapters 1–2: Psalms about Father and Son show Yeshua's exalted nature.*

» *Chapters 3–4: Texts about Israel's wilderness struggle with faith encourage messianics to press on.*

» *Chapters 5–7: Lessons from Melchizedek and the priesthood of Yeshua offer peace to troubled messianics.*

» *Chapter 8: The New Covenant prophecy affirms that*

Torah would be expanded just as has happened in Yeshua.

» *Chapters 9–10: Texts on Tabernacle, sacrifice, and forgiveness offer peace to those who trust in Yeshua.*

» *Chapter 11: The example of biblical characters offers peace to those troubled by the delay in seeing messianic fulfillment.*

» *Chapters 12–13: Practical wisdom, Torah, and call to persevere.*

But all of these principles lead to an important question: does Hebrews know its stuff or does it handle these methods badly? The book of Hebrews may be the key in the way I will develop the connections between Torah theology of atonement and the meaning of Messiah's death. Hebrews is filled with such connections, or priestly mysteries, as I call them. Can we trust these priestly mysteries to be valid and useful for understanding how God purifies us and elevates us to himself?

Does Hebrews Err Concerning the Most Holy Place?

In describing the sanctuary in chapter 9, the author seems to make a mistake. Some commentators snidely remark that the author, being a Jew outside the land of Israel, knows nothing about the Temple in Jerusalem and has made a factual error. What is this alleged mistake? It is the notion from 9:4 that the "golden altar of incense" is "behind the second curtain" in the "Most Holy Place."

Yet this is not true, as the Tabernacle chapters of Exodus reveal. The incense altar was in front of the second curtain (the veil) in the Holy Place and not in the inner chamber (Holy of Holies or Most Holy Place).

When I first encountered this problem, I thought the solution was simple. The writer was speaking about where the incense altar was on Yom Kippur (the Day of Purgation) and not on ordinary days. According to Leviticus, during the Purgation Rite incense is brought into the inner chamber. A close examination, however, shows it was brought in with a portable censer and not by bringing in the whole incense altar (see Leviticus 16:12–13 and the discussion in detail in Milgrom, 1991). Just as in Numbers 16:46, incense can be offered on a portable censer pan (with a handle).

But has the writer truly made a mistake? Actually, no. In fact, the writer of Hebrews seems to exhibit knowledge of the Temple that even many modern scholars lack. First of all, there are important connections between the Ark and the incense altar (especially on Yom Kippur) that should give us a second thought. Second of all, a little knowledge of obscure Temple history can help us out:

> » *The high priest does "make atonement" on the horns of the incense altar at Yom Kippur (Exodus 30:10).*

> » *The high priest does sprinkle blood on the incense altar on Yom Kippur when he atones for the "tent of meeting" (the outer sanctuary) with the goat's blood (Milgrom says "do the same for the Tent of meeting" means daubing blood on the incense altar, as per Leviticus 4:6–7).*

> » *Thus it is significant that the Ark and incense altar are both sprinkled on Yom Kippur (whereas the sprinkling on the outer altar is a common occurrence).*

> » *According to a legend in 2 Maccabees 2:4–8, the prophet Jeremiah carefully hid the Ark and incense altar in a cave (presumably they are connected as two especially potent places for atonement).*

> » *A similar story, different version, is found in 2 Baruch 6:7, in which Jeremiah's scribe, Baruch, sees an angel descend into the Holy of Holies and bring out a number of items, including the incense altar and Ark. It is quite possible that 2 Baruch, like Hebrews, understands something about the change from Tabernacle to Temple (see the next point).*

» *And most decisively, there is excellent reason to believe that in the First Temple (and perhaps the Second) the incense altar was in the inner chamber. 1 Kings 6:22 says that when Solomon built the Temple, he placed an altar in the inner sanctuary, meaning the incense altar. It seems Hebrews had it right after all.*

» *Furthermore, and for those who like obscure theories which just may be correct, Richard Elliott Friedman theorizes (with much evidence) that the original Tabernacle was smaller than typically thought (six by twenty cubits). He says Solomon spaced the giant cherub statues inside his twenty by twenty Shrine to be tall enough and far enough apart that the Tabernacle fit under the wings of these cherub statues (not to be confused with the cherub statues on the Ark cover [atoning place] itself). This theory all the more supports what the writer of Hebrews says. The inner sanctuary of the First Temple likely had the incense altar and the Ark (see Friedman, Who Wrote the Bible?, 174–187).*

As I said at the beginning of the chapter, I had read that Hebrews was a bungled attempt to marry Leviticus theology with Christian doctrine. Supposedly, it is by a Hellenistic (Greek-speaking) author with little facility in the Hebrew Bible. Yet regarding a confusing issue (was the incense altar in the inner chamber?), Hebrews knows better than most modern commentators (even Bruce got this one, in my opinion, wrong).

Someone might object: "but this doesn't mean the incense altar was inside the inner chamber in the Second Temple." Of course not. Hebrews 9 is not about the Second Temple (in which there was no Ark, either, since it was lost before 586 BCE, when the Babylonians destroyed the First Temple). Also, there is no evidence (see Bruce on this) that the writer of Hebrews lived in Jerusalem and had any firsthand knowledge of priestly procedures and details. His (or her) knowledge of the Temple is from scripture, Jewish writings outside of scripture, and perhaps from oral teachings in the synagogue that we may or may not know of in later rabbinic writings.

Hebrews, it seems, knows its stuff. Hebrews brings together Torah and Messiah in new ways. Hebrews connects the meaning of priesthood and atonement in Torah with the meaning of Messiah's death, resurrection, enthronement, and second coming. Hebrews is filled with reflection on priestly mysteries. These priestly mysteries concern our peace with God now and in the world to come. Thankfully, we have in the unknown writer of Hebrews an able guide to these most important issues.

Chapter 6
Hebrews and Priestly Mysteries

Are there mysteries in the Bible? Can there be an implied theology in ritual and actions? Is it possible, by putting together patterns of explicit statements and implicit symbolisms, to read these mysteries?

F.F. Bruce says the writer of Hebrews sees "details" about the sanctuary and priestly procedures as mysteries revealed by the Holy Spirit signifying "spiritual truths for the present time" (27). The book is full of priestly mysteries and sacrificial riddles. The more you know the ways of offerings, consecrating and purging things, the principles of purification laws, the inner workings of priestly duties, the more you can grasp the way Hebrews connects Temple and Messiah, Sinai and New Covenant, the former promises and the better ones.

Being a homily, Hebrews is not intended as an exhaustive treatise. The intent of the book is persuasion, to urge some Jews not to abandon Yeshua and their ties to the messianic community. In the synagogues of the Roman Empire, worship of a person is unacceptable. Even if their ideas of Yeshua's identity as Messiah could be accepted, the messianic communities' choice to worship him sounds like blasphemy. Unless it's true.

Using a number of themes, including the idea of Messiah's supremacy and divinity, the writer calls his audience to hang on to what they have attained in Messiah. The priestly mysteries are not the only theme of the book. But they are of particular interest for understanding Yeshua and atonement.

Someone, a man or a woman, living in a time when the Temple was still in operation—even though he or she apparently had little firsthand knowledge of its organization and politics—and who was around during an era of living knowledge about things like atonement and purifications, wrote about the meaning of these mysteries. We should stand (or sit) and take notice. What Hebrews has to say should be of more interest to us than the opinions of later Christian teachers who did not know the Hebrew Bible so intimately (and who understood sacrifice very poorly from their Greco-Roman background).

The book of Hebrews discusses some priestly mysteries. These are mysteries which could and should occur to those living within the time of the functioning Temple. The benefit of hindsight, of Yeshua's own teaching about his death (see chapter 10, "Yeshua and His Death"), makes it easier by the time of Hebrews to see these mysteries, but some of them were evident already before Yeshua came into the world:

1. *In the Temple, atonement works only because God says it does, which Hebrews points out in various ways by discussing the fallibility of the priests and the limited effectiveness of the offerings. Atonement is by divine decree, not by something inherent in the rituals or elements. The process works because God teaches it to the people, but it is carried out by men and its effects are invisible. This observation leads to the next two.*

2. *The methods of purification have no power in themselves.*

3. *The mediators appointed are fallible like us.*

4. *Temple atonement still left the people outside of the Temple, with God hidden and separated from the people two rooms away. As Hebrews says, "the way into the holy places is not yet opened as long as the first section is still standing" (9:8).*

5. *Scripture reveals another priesthood, pre-dating the Levitical, and transcending it in importance.*

6. *Thus, within scripture, there is foreshadowed a change in the Torah about priesthood. This is to say the ultimate idea of priesthood is something far beyond the Levitical in scope and breadth.*

7. *This indicates something beyond the Temple will come.*

8. *Scripture teaches better purifications than were made in the Temple: Hearts will be circumcised says Deuteronomy. Hearts of stone will be replaced with flesh and God's Spirit placed within as the people are cleansed with water and transformed into keepers of Torah, according to Ezekiel. Torah will be written on the heart, says Jeremiah, and all men will know God.*

9. *The Temple purifications are shadows cast from the radiance of the Glory to come. They are not "mere shadows" and there is no "but" or "only" in the Greek text. To see a shadow cast by the light of his Glory is never something to be modified by words like "mere." What Hebrews points out is that Torah is a signpost pointing to a reality not yet revealed, something implied rather than stated, and something left a mystery for quite some time (an ideal world to come, a total purification of the person, an eternal dwelling).*

10. *So, to summarize all these, what came before prepared the people to receive the greater light of Messiah, who himself cast the shadows from the radiance of his Glory.*

How will these mysteries, discussed in Hebrews, lead us to a deeper understanding of Yeshua as our atonement? They definitely will, but first there is another potential roadblock—is Hebrews supersessionist (a book about Judaism being replaced by the new faith in Yeshua)?

Not Replacement, but Expansion and Improvement

I frequently get challenged by people who don't accept the paradigm of Messianic Judaism (the movement in which I am a rabbi). The idea of Jewish followers of Yeshua keeping Torah and doing so in unity with the larger Jewish community seems heretical to some people. They bring up Hebrews a great deal. They read Hebrews as urging replacement, out with the old and in with the new. The old is obsolete. It seems as simple as that. Or is it?

I think people, since the earliest church fathers whose writings survive, have been mistaken about what was "insufficient" and "obsolete" in Torah. For those who would like an informed discussion of the beginnings of Christian triumphalism over the Jewish people (supersessionism, replacement theology), I recommend R. Kendall Soulen's *The God of Israel and Christian Theology*.

People seem to think God purposefully gave a "bad" Torah. This idea is strongly expressed in the church fathers (Israel sinned and God added burdensome and even cruel regulations). The Temple regulations were supposedly dark and frightening, a terrible religion for any God to require of his people. Pop-preachers today love to ridicule Judaism (I've heard it personally from large pulpits) as a ridiculous system of six hundred and thirteen rules nobody could possibly remember or keep. Thank God Jesus came and reduced the six hundred and thirteen to only two! (Never mind that the two he said were most important are also the hardest two to keep, or that it's really not that hard to choose the turkey sandwich over the ham).

There is a perfect illustration from our culture of what I think Hebrews is actually saying. Since there is no reason to believe the good God would give a bad Torah (a dark, demanding, unyielding law), we need an illustration of a new thing that does not cancel or contradict the old thing it came from; software. When you buy version 2.0 you are not saying version 1.0 had nothing good in it. Why would you buy 2.0 if 1.0 was awful? You see, 2.0 is an expansion of 1.0 and includes the functionality of 1.0 within it. If you already have 1.0, you only need an upgrade. And the upgrade won't work if you uninstall 1.0. The New Covenant is an upgrade to the Abrahamic and Sinai Covenants, and you must retain the first ones to benefit from the later covenant.

I propose that in every case in Hebrews, the issue is that 1.0 (the way his/her Jewish audience practiced their faith before knowing Yeshua) has been greatly improved by 2.0 (the better promises, the way into the holiest place being open, the better priest, etc.). If the old priests were bad, why would we simply want a better version of something bad? The old priests were doing something good. Yeshua is doing something best. It is expansion and improvement, not replacement. Once 2.0 comes out, it is as if 1.0 is obsolete. Once Yeshua has improved the position of the audience of Hebrews, why would they go back to the old version? So it happens that 1.0 (the old) is insufficient by itself (minus the new).

Insufficiency of the Old (By Itself)

Yeshua is "superior to angels" and his name is "is more excellent than theirs" (1:4). So says the writer. He or she is appealing to peers, to those who, like the writer, lived Torah without Yeshua before. Yet now that Yeshua is here, are the angels from the old glory of Torah suddenly bad? Nothing here suggests than angels or the exaltedness of angels is a bad thing.

Yeshua is "counted worthy of more glory than Moses" and yet Moses is not being criticized, for he "was faithful in all God's house as a servant, to testify to the things that were to be spoken later" (3:3–5). It was impossible to think that "perfection had been attainable through the Levitical priesthood" (7:11). After all it was necessary "for another priest to arise after the order of Melchizedek, rather than one named after the order of Aaron" (7:11). Yet Aaron is spoken of in glowing terms. The priests were chosen "to act on behalf of men in relation to God" and "deal gently with the ignorant and wayward" (5:1–2). A true priest should be "called by God, just as Aaron was" (5:4). Moses and Aaron were both good. Yeshua is better. Improvement; not replacement.

Yeshua is a better priest for many reasons, for his appointment is "not on the basis of a legal requirement concerning bodily descent" but "by the power of an indestructible life" (i.e., the resurrection of his body, 7:15). And here many readers, using their replacement presuppositions miss the fact that Hebrews says something startling, but true: "a former commandment is set aside" so that "a better hope is introduced, through which we draw near to God" (7:18–19). With regard to what is he/she saying a former commandment is set aside? Is it when Yeshua came?

No, it is when in Psalm 110, David revealed another version of the priesthood "after the order of Melchizedek." David believed in the sanctuary worship and was even zealous for it. But he also believed in a king-priest of the type of Melchizedek who preceded him in Jerusalem. The covenant of God with David has echoes through time to Messiah. The former commandment set aside is the restriction of the priesthood to the Levitical type. By the Spirit God revealed there was also another kind. Improvement; not replacement. The Levitical priesthood continued to function and certainly Yeshua spoke well of it (Matthew 23:19; Luke 2:49; John 2:16). And it happened before Yeshua came!

A change in priesthood means "there is necessarily a change in the law as well" (7:12). Many readers are quick to read this as though when Yeshua came the Torah was to be allegorized, spiritualized away. This has nothing to do with the message of Hebrews. The "law" changed before Yeshua came, when the Spirit revealed the ongoing priesthood of the Davidic kings. And it is not unusual when circumstances change for the leaders of Israel to adapt Torah to new realities (such as the way David and Solomon changed the function of the Levites). But this has nothing to do with rendering the entire Torah or the entire priestly system invalid. David and the prophets continued to affirm the Levitical priesthood in spite of the different priestly role of the Davidic kings.

The argument continues. Yeshua "has obtained a ministry that is as much more excellent than the old" as the covenant he mediates is better (8:6). Hebrews then cites the new covenant prophecy of Jeremiah 31. The new covenant passage says the new one will not be like the old one. A careless reader will think it must have nothing in common with the old one. But it turns out the new contains the old, as it says "I will put my laws into their minds, and write them on their hearts" (Hebrews 8:10). Which laws? The ones that are in the old covenant! Incidentally, Ezekiel says the same in his parallel promise. When the new heart and Spirit are given and the old taken out that God will "cause you to walk in my statutes and be careful to obey my rules" (Ezekiel 36:27).

So, when Hebrews says "if that first covenant had been faultless, there would have been no occasion to look for a second" (8:7) we need not read it that the first covenant was worthless. It was insufficient and needed something added. Likewise, when Hebrews says in "speaking of a new covenant, he makes the first one obsolete" (8:13) it could easily and consistently mean the same thing: that the first is obsolete without the upgrade. Version 1.0 is obsolete in comparison with 2.0.

Better Promises: Better Priest, Heavenly Zion

Some of the priestly mysteries already alluded to in this chapter are a key to understanding the better promises Hebrews finds in Yeshua than in Torah. Part of his argument, a very legitimate part, is that the insufficiencies of the old Temple and priestly worship would have been evident to forward-thinking, devout Israelites who sought more (as Moses sought "more glory").

Yeshua is fully human and capable of failure just like the old priests (2:10-18). This was necessary so we could know him as sympathetic and understanding, one of us lifting us up to draw near to divinity (what a mediator-priest does). Yet he is superior to the old priests because:

» *He is without any sin or guilt (7:26-27).*

» *His "failure" was not a moral failure, but a deliberate course set to be killed by evil rulers; a deliberate offering of himself (7:27).*

» *The old priests were mortal; Yeshua is immortal (7:23–24).*

» *The old priests were incapable of exaltation, but Yeshua has been raised to the throne in heaven (7:26).*

» *They had to be atoned for, but he atones for all and needs no atonement himself (7:27).*

» *Their weakness was the same human condition we all share (7:21, 28).*

» *He is a better priest all the way around (7:23–28).*

The promises of the atonement Yeshua offers are better by far. The offerings of the old priests do not change the person (9:9). It was impossible for those offerings to remove what truly ails us (10:4). This, in fact, is what the Torah itself teaches about atonement in the sanctuary. The offerings of Leviticus did not cleanse the person; they purified the sanctuary (I will finally spell this out in chapters 8 and 9). The way to the holiest place was closed off and the people were left standing on the other side of a barrier between themselves and God (9:8). Their offerings had to be made repeatedly because, in truth, they were a limited measure, a way to keep God's Presence near, and a sign of something better (10:1–4). But Yeshua made a better atonement.

The first covenant showed signs of its insufficiency. The intended audience of Hebrews should be able to perceive how the Torah itself hints more is available, that more would come. The people of God would not be left forever separated by a barrier, constantly purifying pollution from their own sin and death just to come somewhat near to the hidden God. Surely this could not be the entirety of what God intended for his people!

Mount Sinai would surely become Mount Zion (12:22). The

shadow from light of Glory (8:5) would become "the city of the Living God" and the "festal gathering" of "innumerable angels" (12:22). The shadows point to the light. It moves forward, from Leviticus and broken history to the atonement to final redemption and consummation. The priestly mysteries of Hebrews will be a guide for us in understanding what atonement truly does for us, not just in the future, but now.

Chapter 7

The Sacrifices of Leviticus

Ignorance about the sacrifices, the animal offerings of the Bible, abounds. Long ago I remember a colleague who got a frantic call from a church. He was a Jewish guy coming to speak about Passover. The church said, "We have to cancel because our board will not allow someone to slaughter a lamb on our property."

They knew enough about Passover to be dangerous but not enough to know Passover itself. Don't Jews kill a lamb every year and put blood on the door?

Many times I have been asked questions like, "How did the Israelites have enough animals to make sacrifices every time they sinned?" Not knowing how the sacrificial system worked, many assume everyone tried to live on the same city block as the Temple so they could walk over two or three times a day and slaughter a lamb for every transgression!

Probably the most persistent misunderstanding is that the animal sacrifices temporarily covered sins (like a red-colored screen) and put off judgment until the real sacrifice of Messiah took sins away. I have heard some very descriptive erroneous reasoning about the blood being applied to the altar and God looking down from heaven being able to see only the blood and not sin. One speaker said this has now changed. God looks down on us and sees "Jesus" instead of our sin. The animal sacrifices, they said, were a temporary "covering" and "Jesus" is a permanent one.

Never mind that "to atone" (from the Hebrew *keePAYR*) means "wipe away, cleanse, purge" and not "cover." Never mind that nothing in Leviticus says the sacrifices cover sin, make the worshipper forgiven, or that God sees the sacrifice and not the offerer. How does it all really work? The actual theology of Leviticus has far more to do with the Glory above the cherubim, the Presence of the holy in the midst of the people of Israel, with drawing near to the Presence, and with keeping the Presence from departing Israel.

When? Where?

The times for Israel's gatherings are explained in Exodus 23 and 34, Leviticus 23, and Deuteronomy 16. The names for the three pilgrim feasts of Israel vary slightly from place to place. But they could simply be summarized as: Passover, Weeks, and Tabernacles (*PAY-sakh, SHAV-oo-oat, soo-KOAT*). The Hebrew names are commonly spelled in English as follows: Pesach, Shavuot, and Sukkot.

All the males are required to appear and are told not to come empty-handed. That is, they were to bring tithes, things vowed to God during the year, and offerings.

In general, barring some emergency need to appear before God, it would be at these festivals that Israelites would bring offerings. Thus we see, for example, Elkanah and Hannah coming annually (it sounds like they did not keep all three festivals, or perhaps all Israel kept only one at that time) to Shiloh (where the Tabernacle was at that time, 1 Samuel 1:3, 21).

Origins: The Chicken or the Egg?

By the time of Torah (whether you think Torah goes back to 1400 or 1200 BCE or perhaps even later in Israel's history), the other peoples of the Near East had been offering animals on altars to deities for thousands of years. Did God give the idea of sacrificing animals to humankind? Or did humankind develop this practice independently? Which came first, the chicken or the egg, the command to sacrifice or the custom of sacrifice?

Some are closed to the idea that God would take up and use a human invention to reveal himself. Some assume God only uses customs he "invents." Yet again and again in scripture we find God's commandments making use of pre-existing customs and re-shaping them to have new meanings. There were tent-sanctuaries before the Tabernacle and some kinds of Near Eastern temples had inner shrines (like the Holy of Holies). Before Torah law-codes of the nations also forbade murder and theft. Egyptians and Assyrians had sphinxes and *kuribu* (cherubim) before the Torah was written. Examples abound of human customs being adapted and of God making himself known through the cultural practices of the time.

Those who feel it necessary to believe that God "invented" the idea of sacrifice attempt to find warrant in the Cain and Abel story. Yet Genesis 4 is strangely silent about any commandment or instructions.

What motivations did people have for offering goats and lambs to various deities? The concepts of sacrifice in the Near East involved numerous theologies about demons and deities, which do not concern us. The Torah in some cases spells out, and in others implies, motivations and meanings for sacrifices to the Lord. Before considering those motivations and meanings, however, it is helpful to consider the five basic types of offering in Israel.

Burnt Offering

The first specific mentions of a burnt offering are in Genesis 8 and 22, the accounts of Noah's offerings and of Abraham preparing to offer up his son. Milgrom says of the burnt offering that "it answers every conceivable emotional and psychological need" (2004, pg. 24). It is the sacrifice par-excellence, the costliest and most meaningful general sacrifice. Milgrom further speculates that "it may originally have been the only sacrifice offered except for the well-being offering" prior to the Tabernacle/Temple (2004, pg. 24.).

In Hebrew it is the *olah* (*oh-LAH*), the "ascending," a reference to the smoke which ascends as it burns on the altar (Milgrom 1991, 172). Milgrom suggests that prior to the Tabernacle/Temple, burnt offerings were completely burned (a whole offering) but in Leviticus the skin was removed and was given to the priest (Leviticus 7:8).

Since Leviticus begins with a description of the procedures for the burnt offering, we learn much about the general topic of sacrifice from the burnt offering itself:

» *The act of bringing an offering is drawing near (to the Presence of God in the inner shrine) since the verb in Leviticus 1:3 means literally "bring near."*

» *The offerer himself (or herself, see Leviticus 12 on women bringing offerings) brought it all the way to the area between the altar and the sanctuary ("the entrance to the Tent") itself (this practice was changed in the Second Temple).*

» *Leviticus 1:3 (with the additional insight gleaned from Malachi 1:8) indicates that the basic function of the burnt offering is to gain favor (acceptance). So it is an entreaty. Milgrom adds the additional evidence that the Purification and Reparation offerings never include the phrase about acceptance, being only about atonement (expiation) and not favor.*

» *Leviticus 1:4 says also that the burnt offering makes atonement (expiates) in addition to bringing favor. The rabbis interpreted the Purification offering as being only for violations of prohibitive commandments and that all other expiations were made with the burnt offering.*

» *Leviticus 1:4 says the offerer leans one of his hands (not both as the high priest does at Yom Kippur) on the head of the animal. Milgrom discusses evidence this indicates a declaration of ownership (as if saying, "this is my gift to God") and not transference of sin (as with the double-hand leaning on the scapegoat, Milgrom 1991, 150–153).*

» *Leviticus 1:5 indicates that the offerer, not the priest, slaughters the animal.*

» *The priest then handles the blood, which is something*

> *only the priest is permitted to do and is a sacred function, dashing it against the altar.*

» *Turtle-doves and pigeons are included (verses 14–17) as an offering for the poor. The exceptionally poor may even offer grain instead of an animal, as the next section will show.*

To summarize, then, burnt offerings were costly, burned whole except for the skin which was given to the priest, and brought for the broad purpose of seeking God's favor and also expiating (making atonement, purging). Much of what we want to know about atonement hinges on the meaning of this verb. Although I have already explained its meaning in chapter 2, I will also comment on it further below (see "What Did They Accomplish?").

Grain Offering

The grain offering (or cereal offering) falls under two categories: an accompaniment (Milgrom's word) to the burnt and well-being offering and an independent, discrete sacrifice (also Milgrom's term) which is a "poor man's burnt offering" (Milgrom 1991, 195). It is a complicated offering with a variety of "recipes" which are either uncooked offerings with frankincense added or cooked offerings without frankincense.

As a poor man's burnt offering, the grain offering can be used in every way like the burnt offering. In Hebrew it is called the *MEEN-khah* (usually spelled *minchah*), which means "gift." Like the burnt offering it is a gift intended to secure God's favor. The grain offering is specifically called for in certain special instances (from Milgrom, 1991, 200; references are as in Jewish Bibles):

» *The thanksgiving offering (Leviticus 7:12–14).*

» *The ordination of the priests (Leviticus 8:26–27).*

» *The Nazirite's offerings (Numbers 6:19–21).*

» *As a Purification offering for a poor man (Leviticus 5:11).*

» *In the case of a wife suspected of adultery (Numbers 5:15–26).*

» *In the daily offering made by the high priest (Leviticus 6:12–16).*

» *The bread of the presence (Leviticus 24:5–9).*

» *Barley firstfruits during Passover (Leviticus 2:14–16; 23:10–11).*

» *Wheat firstfruits on Shavuot (Leviticus 23:15–17).*

Grain offerings were originally burned whole, but the priestly laws changed this practice. Only a token was burned and the rest was given to the priest(s) (Leviticus 2:3; 6:10; 24:9). There are questions about how early or late this law was added to Torah since the practice of Israelites like Manoah (Judges 13:19–20) and even in Solomon's time (1 Kings 8:64) was to burn them.

The grain offering is an exception to the general rule that atonement requires death and blood. If the grain offering was a poor man's burnt offering, then it also made atonement. While atonement is not mentioned in Leviticus 2, it is mentioned in the poor man's Purification offering, which was a grain offering, in Leviticus 5:11.

Well-Being Offering

Variously translated as peace offering or fellowship offering, the well-being offering means a sacrifice "whose meat is eaten by the worshiper" (Milgrom 1991, 218). It is called a *ZE-vakh sh'lammeem* (*zevach shelammim*), a "slain offering for well-being." The word *shelammim* is related to the familiar word *shalom*:

peace, wholeness, and well-being.

Well-being offerings include many subcategories and special instances:

» *Freewill offerings (Leviticus 7:16).*

» *Vow (or votive) offerings (Leviticus 7:16).*

» *Thanksgiving offerings (Leviticus 7:11–15).*

» *Some Israelites conceived of an annual offering (1 Samuel 1:21).*

» *Some clans brought clan offerings (1 Samuel 20:29).*

» *The Passover lamb (Exodus 12:23; 23:18; 34:25; Deuteronomy 16:2–4).*

Milgrom says all of these offerings have in common rejoicing before the Lord (see Deuteronomy 12:7, 12, 18; 14:26; 16:11, 14). There were laws about eating the worshiper's portion of the sacred meat within a certain period of time. Meat from a well-being offering left too long was considered "tainted" (both literally and more importantly, ritually, Leviticus 7:18; 19:7; Isaiah 65:4). A person had to be in a state of ritual purity to eat the sacred meat (Leviticus 7:19–20, see chapter 4, "Ritual Pollution: Sin and Death"). Some types of well-being offerings were forbidden to non-Israelites (Passover, Exodus 12:45, 48).

Thanksgiving offerings must have been in response to some blessing from God, such as recovery from illness or a similar rescue. Votive (vow) offerings were made in fulfillment of a vow (such as, "Lord, deliver me from this and I will bring you a lamb"). Freewill offerings cover the general offerings brought for rejoicing at festivals and similar occasions. Although Deuteronomy makes provision for slaughtering meat without offering any portion at the sanctuary (Deuteronomy 12:21), when coming to the sanctuary, all festive meat was offered as a well-being offering with portions given to the priests (7:28–36).

Purification Offering

Most translations call this the sin offering. Yet this offering is required in a number of matters that do not involve any transgression: childbirth (Leviticus 12), the end of a Nazirite vow (Numbers 6), cleansing from scale disease ("leprosy," Leviticus 14:19), and the dedication of Israel's altar (Leviticus 8:15, Milgrom 1991, 253). It is really a matter of purification.

Before there was a central sanctuary (Tabernacle/Temple), there was no need for a sacrifice like the purification offering. Its purpose is purifying the place of Israel's worship, which is the place of God's Presence. It cleanses the Temple, not the worshipper. The burnt offering also has this function, yet its cleansing function is non-specific. In many specific cases the purification offering is mandated in Torah.

Key verses for understanding the purification offering include Leviticus 15:31 and Numbers 19:20 (JPS):

You shall put the Israelites on guard against their unclean-ness, lest they die through their uncleanness by defiling My Tabernacle which is among them.

If anyone who has become unclean fails to cleanse himself, that person shall be cut off from the congregation, for he has defiled the Lord's sanctuary. The water of lustration was not dashed on him: he is unclean.

The transgressions of the people as well as their ritual im-purities (not sin) create dirt which travels like air pollution and defiles God's sanctuary, where his Presence is enshrined in the invisible throne above the cherubim (see chapter 3, "The Divine

Glory Above the Cherubim"). It is not a sin to become impure. But it is a sin not to follow the purification procedures. Some serious types of impurity require a purification offering. Inadvertent transgression of prohibitive commandments also requires a purification offering (Leviticus 4:2).

Ezekiel 11:22 and Lamentations 2:7 illustrate the need for the purification offering (Milgrom 1991, 258). Ezekiel, from Babylon, saw a vision of the divine Glory departing from the Temple before the Babylonians destroyed it. The poet of Lamentations described the ruin of the Temple as "The Lord has scorned his altar, disowned his sanctuary" (ESV). Milgrom says, "God will not abide in a polluted sanctuary" and "if the pollution continues to accumulate, the end is inexorable" (258).

With most purification offerings, the blood is applied to the altar, like the blood is applied in other offerings. In these instances of the purification offering, the meat is eaten by the priests. Yet for certain more serious situations, the blood is applied to the incense altar inside the Holy Place and sprinkled before the veil (Leviticus 4:6–7, 13–21). When the blood is applied to the inner altar, the meat must be burned outside the camp (Leviticus 4:11–12). The meat for this type of offering may not be eaten (Leviticus 6:23, which is 6:30 in Christian Bibles). Blood is brought to the inner altar for more serious matters, such as a sin of the priest or ruler or the entire community. These sins pollute inside the sanctuary whereas the sins of the common individuals pollute only the outer altar (with the exception of un-repented sins and un-cleansed impurities, for which the Yom Kippur rite is required).

The purification offering is the cleansing ritual of choice for the Temple. It is common and its performance is an absolute requirement in many circumstances. It is not a voluntary offering in any sense.

Reparation Offering

The transition from the purification offering to the reparation offering can be confusing for several reasons. First, there is a sort of appendix to the purification offerings dealing with some special cases (Leviticus 5:1–13). This section Milgrom calls the "graduated purification offering," since the cost of the offerings is graduated by the economic status of the offender. Unfortunately, many translations interpret a word as "guilt offering" in 5:6 and 5:7 which would be better rendered "penalty" or "compensation." Add to this the fact that there is not a chapter break at 5:14, where the reparation offering begins and it is hard to tell how the subject has changed. The JPS and ESV translations both handle the details quite well but many others do not. As if all of these confusions were not enough, Jewish and Christian Bibles differ on where to divide the chapter. Therefore, I will provide the following outline to clarify what belongs where:

» *The graduated purification offering (Leviticus 5:1–13).*

» *The reparation offering (Leviticus 5:14–6:7 in Christian Bibles; 5:14–26 in Jewish Bibles).*

Most translations call this the guilt offering, but it is actually a compensation or penalty for a violation that involves sacrilege. Milgrom translates Leviticus 5:15, "When a person commits a sacrilege by being inadvertently remiss with any of the Lord's sancta, he shall bring as his penalty to the Lord a ram without blemish . . ." (319). The penalty paid to God is a separate matter from any restitution that must be paid to persons who were defrauded. The reparation in the phrase "reparation offering" is paid to God. In the matter of some kinds of sacrilege there may also be a payment of money to the sanctuary (such as a failure to bring all of the tithe or something vowed to God that has monetary value). Otherwise the reparation is the ram that is offered as payment for the sin.

A sacrilege (JPS uses the word "trespass" and ESV uses the phrase "breach of faith") involves misusing a holy object, something dedicated to the Lord's use. Another type of sacrilege is a violation of an oath sworn by God's name. Finally, a third type of sacrilege is defrauding and abusing other people, which causes not only damage between the offender and offended, but also is a sacrilege against God.

In all of these cases, some of them even deliberate violations of prohibitive commandments ("you shall not swear a false oath," "you shall not steal"), reparation must be made to God for the sacrilege. The purification offering will not do in such cases.

What Did They Accomplish?

The effects of sacrifices are multiple. Different types of offerings were brought for different situations. A simple list of what the sacrifices did and did not accomplish might be a good way to start, followed by an explanation of some of the language used for sacrifice:

> » *They could acquire God's favor for you.*

> » *They could increase the power of your prayer.*

> » *They enabled you to draw near to God's Presence, by literally enabling you to approach the altar and be near the sanctuary in which God's Glory was enthroned.*

> » *They purified whatever pollution you and your family had caused to defile God's altar.*

> » *They could make reparation to God for a sacrilege.*

> » *They did not, however, cause you to be free from guilt before God, cleansed personally from all your sins, or forgiven by God in his heavenly court.*

When the Torah describes what the sacrifices accomplished, the language used must be translated and interpreted carefully. A great deal of carelessness and failure to comprehend the entire system of offerings, purity laws, and the divine Presence has led to misunderstanding.

A person brings a burnt offering (same with grain offering) to come near to God's Presence as indicated by the verb for bringing an offering which means "bring near" (Leviticus 1:3). This nearness is literal (you are nearer the sanctuary when bringing an offering than at any other time) and figurative (you are near in your thoughts and emotions to God by this experience).

> » *A person brings a burnt offering (same with grain offering) to be accepted (to acquire favor) before the Lord (Leviticus 1:3). It is God's acceptance and favor that is being sought. The expression "for his acceptance" is not used with the purification and reparation offerings, whose purpose is only atonement.*

> » *He also brings the burnt offering (same with grain offering) if he needs expiation (cleansing). This is a separate purpose from seeking favor. His offering will be "accepted on his behalf to atone for him" or "to expiate for him" (Leviticus 1:4, to purge or cleanse). The animal on which he leaned his hand is accepted for the purpose he brought it to accomplish. If he is seeking atonement (the cleansing of defilement he has caused) it will atone that defilement.*

> » *"Atone" in Leviticus 1:4 (variously translated "to expiate," "to atone," "to make atonement," etc.) is an important word to study in building a theology of Leviticus. Milgrom notes that in biblical poetry it is used synonymously with "wipe" and "remove" (Jeremiah 18:23; Isaiah 27:9; Milgrom 1991, 1,079). In other texts dealing with purifications it is used with "purify" and "decontaminate" (Leviticus 14:48, 52, 58). Milgrom discusses and discards the notions of "cover" and "ransom" from the use of "atone" in general sacrificial contexts (1,082-1,083). Therefore, when sacrificial blood is dashed it is a cleansing agent decontaminating the altar from the defilement caused by the worshiper and his family from the last festival until now. The phrase "to atone" does not mean "to render the*

worshiper (and his family) free from all guilt before God."

» *In a number of contexts with the purification and reparation offerings we read that the effect of the offering is "he will be forgiven" (4:20, 26, 31, 35; 5:10, 13, 16, 18). In none of these contexts does it seem that someone is "forgiven for all their sins" and judged guilt-free before God in all things. Rather, the meaning seems to be "forgiven for the defilement he caused" or "for the sacrilege" so that the relationship is restored. The person is able to worship and be accepted by God. This is comparable to the difference between a person asking God's forgiveness in prayer (ongoing forgiveness in one's relationship) and the larger matter of being freed from all consequences of transgression which I believe to be part of the purpose of Messiah's death (ultimate forgiveness).*

» *A votive (vow) offering is brought as a fulfillment of a promise made to God, often with the intent of seeking his aid ("if you help, I will offer"). Thus, one of the effects of offering is to strengthen the power of prayer and more strongly seek God's help.*

Hebrews and Leviticus Agree

In the Temple, says Hebrews, "sacrifices are offered that cannot perfect the conscience of the worshiper" (9:9). F.F. Bruce insightfully comments on Hebrews 9:9, "Animal sacrifice . . . could accomplish at best a ceremonial and symbolical removal of pollution" (*The Epistle to the Hebrews*, 210). The "perfecting the conscience" that Messiah accomplishes is the knowledge that our guilt is totally eliminated. No one thought an animal offering was sufficient to free us from guilt in God's court and bring ultimate forgiveness. Therefore the worshiper's conscience before God was still strained and ashamed.

Hebrews also says about the Levitical sacrifices, "It is impossible for the blood of bulls and goats to take away sins" (10:4).

That is, they did not remove the blameworthiness of the worshiper but only the contamination that he or she caused to defile God's sanctuary. By contrast, the death of Messiah affects sanctification for his followers, making us holy or elevated to the proper status to dwell with the Holy One (10:10). No one claimed the offerings at the Temple performed such a feat. The worshiper was shut out of the Temple, permitted only outside its doors.

How Do They Relate to Yeshua?

This is a more complicated question than it might first appear. Many simply assume that the death of Messiah is a replacement for the system of animal offerings in the Temple. A simple check of what we have learned should reveal the error in this assumption. Is the death of Yeshua like a burnt offering, a grain offering, a well-being offering, a purification offering, or a reparation offering? He was not burned and was in no way comparable to the grain offering. Some might make a case that Christian communion or Eucharist services are a sort of new well-being offering (but there would be serious objections to raise here also). Yeshua's death was not about purifying the Temple nor was it limited to matters of sacrilege.

The sacrifices of Leviticus really have a different meaning and set of purposes from the death of Messiah. Perhaps this is why the apostles continued bringing offerings in the Temple during the early days of the Yeshua movement. Such was the practice of James and Paul as well as others in Acts 21:21–26. The Nazirite vow involved a burnt, grain, well-being, and purification offering. Thus, Paul offered and paid for others to offer all of these kinds of sacrifices. The Temple was still the place of God's Holiness. It still needed to be kept clean from defilement. Well-being offerings still could be eaten in rejoicing at the Temple. The purpose of the Temple offerings was not fulfilled in Yeshua's death. His death did something else entirely.

Chapter 8

The Divine Glory Incarnate

The Spirit of God brooded over the primeval waters in the creation story. The spoken word of God ("Let there be") entered the world and made everything that is. God walked in the Garden with Adam and Eve. Abraham was visited by two angels in human form and the Judge of all the earth himself, also in human form. Jacob saw the angelic beings going between earth and the heavens on a staircase. The Presence of God in different forms with varying intensity was known to appear and act on earth.

A theophany is the appearance of some aspect of God's being, coming from the alternate reality of the heavenly into this reality, the temporal and earthly. A theophany sometimes becomes more than an appearance. If an appearance remains, it becomes an indwelling; a dwelling of God in the midst of the people. A theophany is an ephemeral appearance; an indwelling is a theophany that remains in the midst of the people. As an indwelling is greater than an appearance, so incarnation is greater than an indwelling.

Incarnation is more than a theophany or an indwelling. It is the idea of the divine dwelling not merely amidst humans, but within a human, joining divinity and humanity together in a singular divine-man. God in a form of hidden Glory appeared to Abraham and Moses (theophany). God in a more intense and abiding form indwelt the Temple in the midst of the people (indwelling). God in Yeshua incarnated himself, took on humanity, and his Glory was hidden in the form of a man (incarnation).

In any theophany the Glory of God is hidden in a form by which he appears: to Abraham as one of three men, to Moses in a fire that did not consume the bush. In any indwelling the Glory of God is hidden in some obscuring enclosure: the fire in the pillar of cloud to Israel in the wilderness, the Glory enthroned above the cherubim which was obscured behind the doors and the veil in the Holy of Holies. In the incarnation divinity is obscured in human form so that he "made himself nothing, taking the form of a servant" (Philippians 2:7, ESV).

Theophanies

When three visitors came to see Abraham, it is not immediately apparent, but two of them are angelic beings and one is an appearance of God. The story begins by saying "The Lord appeared to him by the terebinths of Mamre" (Genesis 18:1, ESV). This is not a separate event, but a summary of what happens next. Three men were coming and Abraham ran to meet them. But were they truly men?

In verse 13, the Lord speaks to Abraham. This also is not a separate event. The Lord is one of the three visitors. In case this is still not apparent to the reader, the Lord speaks to himself (internally) in verse 17 and out loud to the whole group of four in verses 20–21. Having decided to go down and see if Sodom deserves judgment, it is two angels (19:1) who actually travel to Sodom while the third visitor, the Lord, remains with Abraham and has a conversation. Abraham is not in the dark about the identity of the visitor. He knows this is God appearing in human form. He addresses him directly as "the Judge of all the earth" (18:25, JPS).

It is not difficult for God to appear in human form. He also appears as fire, storm, and unbearable light. Moses sees "an angel of the Lord" in a flame that does not consume a bush (Exodus 3:2). The one speaking to Moses from the bush is called simply "the Lord" and "God" (3:4). Is this an angel (messenger) of the Lord or the Lord himself? Perhaps we may say a theophany is both the Lord himself and a messenger from the Lord.

The abode of God and earth are separate realities. God's dwelling is eternal and boundless; earth is temporal and bounded. "The heavens to their uttermost reaches cannot contain" God (1 Kings 8:27). Yet God can appear in the earthly realm in various forms, including a human form.

A theophany is temporary. Usually a theophany is brief. When it is over, the divine Presence is gone. Yet one theophany was more enduring. The cloud-encased pillar of fire in the wilderness filled the Tabernacle (Exodus 40:34–38). The Glory was enthroned (invisibly) above the cherubim in the inner shrine (Holy of Holies). What was a theophany became an indwelling.

Indwellings

"Let them make Me a sanctuary that I may dwell among them," said God to Moses (Exodus 25:8, JPS). In the wilderness encampment, the regulations for ritual purity were even higher than they would be normally when the people lived in the land. God gave strict purity commands "so that they do not defile the camp of those in whose midst I dwell" (Numbers 5:3, JPS).

The responsibility of a human encountering a mere theophany is reverence. Moses was commanded to remove his sandals (Exodus 3:5). The Israelites, without needing a command, fell on their faces in fear when God appeared at the Tabernacle inauguration (Leviticus 9:24).

The responsibility of the people when there is an indwelling of the Glory is even greater. The whole system of purity laws is about this (see chapter 4, "Ritual Pollution: Sin and Death"). The Israelites must not allow God's sanctuary to be defiled (Leviticus 15:31). They must follow purification procedures for themselves and their clothing so as not to defile God's dwelling on earth (Numbers 19:20). They must cleanse the altar continually and the inner shrine once a year at least with blood as the ritual detergent. The blood cleanses or wipes away the defilement or pollution caused by the proximity of death and sin to God's Glory.

The heavenly abode of God is a place without death. The ideal world to come will be without sin. If God is to dwell in the midst of the people, sin and human death are repugnant to him. If the people ignore purifications and sacrifices, if the people do not follow the Torah in faithfulness to God, his Glory will depart. "My soul will abhor you" and "the land will vomit you out," says God

(Leviticus 26:30; 18:28, ESV). Ezekiel watched the Glory depart from the Temple in Jerusalem in a vision (Ezekiel 10). Yet he also saw that it would return in the last days (Ezekiel 43).

Glory in Theophanies and Indwellings

That there are varying degrees of intensity in theophanies and indwellings should be apparent. The experience of Israel and Moses with theophanies and indwellings makes this evident.

All Israel saw the theophany in the pillar of fire encased in cloud (Exodus 13:20–21). Sometimes the Glory appeared to the people in other ways, such as showing up in the courtyard of the Tabernacle at its inauguration (Leviticus 9:23–24). The people were able to bear this degree of Glory, though in Leviticus 9 they were frightened and fell on their faces.

Moses clearly saw levels or intensities of Glory beyond what other Israelites could bear. God spoke with him "face to face" (Exodus 33:11). Yet Moses asked for a theophany of even greater intensity, "Please, show me your glory" (33:18, ESV). The people could not bear even the afterglow of the Glory from Moses' face, "the people of Israel saw Moses, and behold, the skin of his face shone, and they were afraid to come near him" (Exodus 34:30, ESV). So Moses would wear a veil until the glow diminished (Exodus 34:33–35).

And there were levels which Moses himself could not bear. When the Glory came down and penetrated the Tabernacle, into the inner shrine (Holy of Holies), Moses had to leave because he could not bear it (Exodus 40:35). In answer to Moses' prayer to see God's Glory in Exodus 33:18, God replied, "you cannot see my face, for man shall not see me and live" (Exodus 33:20, ESV). Elaborate measures were taken to shield Moses from the full intensity: he was hidden in a crack in the rock, God covered the crack with his "hand," and passed by with his "back" toward Moses (Exodus 33:22–23).

Therefore, there were levels of radiance in manifestations

of God's being. They ranged from those veiled enough for all the people to see, those which frightened the people, those which Moses experienced, greater ones he desired to experience, those which Moses could not bear, and even those which would kill Moses if not greatly obscured by multiple means.

How greatly could a manifestation of God be intensified? Could something "greater than the Temple" come? Could God hide his Glory in a form which humans could see and touch?

Those who became convinced that Yeshua was more than a theophany, more than a person with an indwelling, had this to say, "No one has ever seen God," which is to say God in his full being (John 1:18, ESV). Yet Yeshua "has made him known" (John 1:18, ESV) and "the Word became flesh and dwelt among us, and we have seen his glory" (John 1:14, ESV). And Yeshua could say, "Whoever has seen me has seen the Father" (John 14:9, ESV).

Incarnation Foreshadowed

The theophanies of the Hebrew Bible and the theme of the indwelling Presence of God in the Temple lead to the possibility that God would increase the joining of the two worlds, the earthly and heavenly. God already broke the barrier between the heavens and earth in each of the theophanies and actions of the Presence on earth. At creation it seems God in his full being remained separate from the created world, but sent some aspects or radiations of his being into the world to shape it.

Thus the word of God entered and created. The Psalmist says, "By the word of the Lord the heavens were made" (Psalm 33:6, JPS). Wisdom, the wisdom of God, was present in the making of all things: "I was there when He set the heavens into place; When He fixed the horizon upon the deep" (Proverbs 8:27, JPS). The "let there be" word emanated from God and made all that is. So the Targum says, "And the Memra (word) of Hashem (the Lord) said, 'Let there be light' and there was light by his Memra" (Targum Neofiti, cited in *The Annotated Jewish New Testament*, page 547, Daniel Boyarin, "Logos, a Jewish Word"). The world came into existence because God from the heavenly realm made a separate reality, the earthly realm exists from heaven with the word of God as the connection between them.

Every theophany is a connection between heaven and earth. In the story of Abraham's three visitors, God sent out from himself in some form a representation of himself which appeared to Abraham to be a man. To Moses in Exodus 3, some aspect of God's being appeared in a fire.

But an indwelling is a more enduring and intense connection between heaven and earth. Israelites came to the Tabernacle and later the Temple to be near the Glory in the inner shrine, enthroned above the cherubim. Where is God's throne, in heaven or on earth? In the case of the Glory dwelling there the answer would seem to be both, simultaneously. The relationship between the Glory and the full being of God in the heavenly realm is a mystery.

And so the idea of incarnation is also an intensification. As an indwelling is more intense than a theophany, so an incarnation is more intense than an indwelling. The indwelling Glory in the Temple joined heaven to a place on earth. The incarnate divine-man Yeshua joined divinity with humanity.

That there would be a miracle as extraordinary as the incarnation is not something we could have deduced beforehand. It is not that the theophanies or indwellings foretold an incarnation. The miracle of the incarnation, rather, is something we understand in hindsight with foreshadowings in the theophanies and indwelling. They were precursors to the incarnation. Yet the incarnation was beyond anything God had promised, an unexpected gift of the highest order.

That God desires to dwell with humans is evident. That there is a separation between God and humanity is also evident. If theophanies were not hidden enough, if they were too intense, people could be harmed or die. The indwelling at the Temple was something people could approach, but not without a separating barrier, continual cleansing, and a whole priesthood to maintain the juncture between people and God in safety. Yet God wanted the people to come near.

At the very least, it seems God intended a closer union between himself and the people than the Temple indwelling allowed. The way it actually happened, as the disciples discovered the mystery that Yeshua was God in the flesh, was the invasion of humanity by deity in a singular divine-man redeemer. More than a theophany and even more than a dwelling Presence, Messiah took the bridge between the heavenly and earthly to the highest level.

In Leviticus God drew near to us to invite us near to him. In the incarnation he became what we are so we could become what he is. In Leviticus the distance between humans and God was made evident. In the incarnation God bridged the distance. In Leviticus the unfitness of humans for union with God required a whole priesthood and system of purifications. In the incarnation, God did what was necessary to incorporate us in Messiah and elevate us with Messiah to union with God.

Scot McKnight on Recapitulation

When we think of atonement and Yeshua, often the death of Messiah, the cross, is where we think all of it happens. Yet the atonement Yeshua brings is far more than most people realize. When the divine Messiah was born, so that God took on humanity and was born as a human, the work of atonement was already started.

In the history of Christian doctrine, the earliest explanation of what Messiah did to bring humanity into union with God was as much about the incarnation as the death of Messiah. And the story of humanity's redemption also could not have happened without the resurrection of the divine Messiah. This early version of atonement theory is known as recapitulation.

To recapitulate something means to repeat it, often by summarizing it. Scot McKnight gives what I think is a full-orbed explanation of how Messiah recapitulated humanity's story: "Jesus recapitulated Adam's life, Israel's life, and the life of every one of us" (*A Community Called Atonement*, 101). The story of what Messiah did is most simply described this way: "Jesus became what we are so that we could become what he is" (110).

This is a multi-layered accomplishment of Messiah. It involves the incarnation, death, and resurrection of Messiah as well as the imparting of the Holy Spirit to Messiah's followers. The story of atonement in the recapitulation mode could be described this way:

> » *Humans (and Adam as representative of humanity) were made as images of the divine being.*
>
> » *Yet humans became damaged and became infected with corruptibility and death.*
>
> » *God took on humanity (became what we are) in order to enable humanity to achieve union with God.*
>
> » *The divine Messiah lived as one also corrupted with death and experienced death as a human (he identified with us "all the way down" says McKnight (110)).*
>
> » *Yet the divine Messiah overcame death through the resurrection and defeated (symbolically?) corruption.*
>
> » *As Adam represented humanity, so also Messiah represented humanity; as Adam dragged humanity down, Messiah raised humanity up.*
>
> » *Messiah experienced and summed up (recapitulated) as a representative what all humanity has experienced, but he was a victor to lead us as a representative to the union we were made for.*

It is important to see that this story could not have taken place without an incarnation. Messiah's death is often called by critics a human sacrifice. A less hostile critic might call his death nothing more than a martyrdom. Even if he was the ideal man, a guiltless person, his death as the most righteous martyr who ever lived would still fall far short of the recapitulation story. Yeshua was, according to this high view of his identity, God taking on humanity and rescuing us from within.

The Hebrew Bible and Recapitulation

In the Torah's system of purity laws and sacrifices, all humans carry a kind of corruption which is called impurity. All people are shut out from God's Presence though God invites the people near. The Glory in the inner shrine expresses God's desire for nearness with us and at the same time our ineligibility to come any nearer.

The Torah promises acceptance, that God will accept the worship of those who keep covenant and bring near their offerings to God. Yet the prophets, starting with Moses, promise a better purification: circumcised hearts, Torah-inscribed hearts, and new hearts (Deuteronomy 30:6; Jeremiah 31:33; Ezekiel 36:26).

How will the bridge between the nearness the Torah/Temple system offered and the greater union the prophets foretold happen? The Hebrew Bible does not say.

When Yeshua came and it was revealed to his followers that he was the divine Messiah, the answers began to dawn on them. The mystery of God bringing union between himself and humanity started to be solved. There is no one story that can contain all of the truth of atonement. It is a story that can and must be told several ways. It is a story that can be pictured with at least five different metaphors (offering, justification, reconciliation, redemption, ransom; McKnight, 38). It is a story that can be told with six different accomplishments of Messiah (recapitulation, victory, satisfaction, substitution, penal substitution, representation). It is a story that involves at least four events (incarnation, death, resurrection, sending the Spirit). It is a story that brings more than personal forgiveness, but the reconciling of all things in Messiah and total union of humans with God in Messiah.

Chapter 9
Metaphors of Divine Atonement

It happens sometimes that married couples, when getting to know new friends, will ask, "How did the two of you meet and fall in love?" I have both asked and been asked this very thing. How can one answer such a question? Do we condense our story down to one simple moment? If so, my response is, "I saw her in a college classroom, a pretty blonde in a purple dress, and was smitten."

If there is one story that I think encapsulates the whole process through which I "met" Linda and fell in love, it would be that one. But there is a whole lot more to it than that. I also observed her ways, her smile, her kindness with people. I became convinced before I was ever fortunate enough to take her on our first date (studying together for that class we had in common) that she was the kind of woman I needed. I also experienced in the first few weeks of dating a connection that I knew was real, a bond that would last a lifetime.

To do actual justice to the story, I would need to describe more than one event in the Derek and Linda saga. I had seen other pretty women before Linda and felt the pangs of romantic attraction. The scene etched in my memory from that college classroom is not the total explanation for what has resulted. Our twenty two years (and counting) of marriage and our eight children together are not completely explicable by that one vision of her.

When it comes to the atonement brought about by Yeshua, though, people often have a one-picture idea in mind. That one picture would be the cross. Perhaps this is because of the famous verse by Paul, "Jews demand signs and Greeks seek wisdom, but we preach Christ crucified" (1 Corinthians 1:22-23, ESV). Or it could be the similar saying, "Far be it from me to boast except in the cross of our Lord Jesus Christ" (Galatians 6:14, ESV).

What we could say, rather than insisting on a one-picture view of atonement, is that the death of Messiah on the cross is a dramatic, pivotal, picturesque moment in the story of atonement. It is easier to conjure an image of the cross than, say, the incarnation. The resurrection is an empty tomb, a less scenic spectacle than the cross. The death of Messiah is moving, an image of one who laid down his life for his friends, a sacrificial deliverer.

But there are many pictures of divine atonement. Just as in any story of meeting the love of your life there are multiple, overlapping scenes, so it is with atonement. Leaning on the work of Scot McKnight, I will describe atonement through five different metaphors (offering, justification, reconciliation, redemption, ransom). And in chapter 10 I will describe it in terms of six accomplishments of Messiah (recapitulation, victory, satisfaction, substitution, penal substitution, representation). And it will encompass four events (incarnation, death, resurrection, sending the Spirit).

Metaphor #1: Offering

On that day when we will approach the shining city and its gates we will hear a voice cry out, "No corruption of death or weight of guilt may enter here." We will quail and our garments which had seemed clean a moment before will now appear as a leper's rags. As we are dejected and about to turn away another voice will cry, "This one has been purified by Messiah's water and blood." In that moment we will be transfigured and our clothes will become white as light and we will enter in.

He was crucified at the time Passover lambs were to be slaughtered. He spoke of laying his life down, of giving himself for his friends. He said the Son of Man must be crucified. His beloved disciple saw the water and blood during the gruesome scene after his passing. The writer of Hebrews describes what Yeshua did by saying "offered for all time a single sacrifice for sins" (Hebrews 10:12). Clearly, many understood the metaphor of sacrifice for the death of Messiah.

Why do I say it is a metaphor? Yeshua was not literally a sacrifice. His throat was not cut. He was not slaughtered in a temple, Roman or Jewish. His blood was not applied to an altar. A human being could not be a kosher sacrifice for Jews nor an acceptable offering for Romans. The actual form of death he suffered was an execution, not a sacrifice. And no animal ever chose itself for sacrifice and laid its life down willingly. Critics of Messiah's atonement often, with no regard for metaphor, claim that Yeshua's death could not be atoning since God rejects human sacrifice.

The meaning of a metaphor should be sought in what one thing has in common with another. No metaphor is perfect. Things and events used in a metaphor or always both like and unlike what they are compared to. McKnight quotes the words of G.B. Caird, "Metaphor is a lens; it is as though the speaker were saying, 'Look through this and see what I have seen, something you never would have noticed without the lens!'" (36).

Sacrifice is not literally what the death of Messiah is all about. It is a lens through which to understand how the death of a man could affect some change in our status. If we look through the lens of the picture of an animal offering, we find points of comparison:

» *The offerings brought worshipers nearer to God.*

» *The offerings purified pollution caused by wrongdoing.*

» *The offerings purified pollution caused by death and the mortality of humans.*

» *The offerings acquired favor (grace) for the worshiper.*

» *The offerings repaired the damage done to relationship with God by sacrilege.*

In truth, the sacrifice metaphor for Messiah's death is inadequate. This is why Hebrews constantly points out the difference between Yeshua's death and its effects on the one hand and the death of rams and bulls in the Temple on the other. Messiah's death was once-for-all, actually perfects the conscience before God, takes away sins, is effective in heaven and not just in an earthly temple, purifies our whole being, and more.

There are also two other kinds of sacrifice besides the Temple offerings to which we might compare Messiah's death: the scapegoat and the Passover lambs in Egypt. The scapegoat in Leviticus 16 has the sins of Israel symbolically transferred upon it and is sent away, removing sins from the vicinity of God and his people. The Passover lambs in Egypt had their blood smeared on doorposts as a protection from divine wrath. No other sacrificial blood functioned that way and yet, if anything, at the Last Supper, this is the primary metaphor Yeshua used for his death.

Sacrifice is a vivid picture of atonement and the only one of the main five which is about a figure dying for the benefit of others. Neither those who accused Yeshua (chief priests), nor those who carried out his death (Roman soldiers), nor those who benefit from Yeshua's death (his followers) offered up Yeshua as a sacrifice to God. We cannot exactly say he sacrificed himself, but rather that he willingly submitted to death. He was a willing victim with no one as the offerer. Yet the metaphor rings true since his death brings union between humans and God, purifies, eliminates guilt, brings favor, protects from wrath, and removes sins.

Metaphor #2: Justification

It will be when we enter the heavenly court we will see the figure of the Judge and tremble before him. Every excuse will flee our imagination and no lies will come to our lips. An angel will begin reviewing before the Judge and his court all of our shameful deeds. Yet another angel will say, "This one is with the people of Messiah and is found

to be in him." Then the Judge himself will stand and say,
"See how this one was changed after being incorporated
into the people of my Son." And so the angelic spokesman
will review the deeds wrought in love for Messiah and his
people and our fear will flee until the Judge says, "Vindi-
cated in my Son."

"Judge not lest you be judged," said Yeshua (Matthew 7:1, ESV). The judge whose verdict we would rather not draw on ourselves could be other people, but it could be God as Judge. Luke's version (6:37) more clearly implies the divine Judge. Yeshua and his Father judge (John 7:15). The metaphor of the divine courtroom is reason to settle with those who have an offense against us (Matthew 5:25). Yeshua used the example of a humble repentant who beat his chest, which is an active pursuit of righteousness, as one who "went down to his house justified" (Luke 18:14). Yeshua spoke of judging nations, of the disciples sitting on thrones judging the tribes of Israel, and of the final day of judgment that is coming.

The image of the courtroom, of God as Judge, and of Yeshua's atonement promising vindication (justification) for his followers is Paul's favorite. "All who believe" are justified by God's grace (his generous mercy) through "the redemption that is in Christ Jesus" (Romans 3:22–23). In the larger saying (Romans 3:21–26) Paul brings up redemption and sacrifice as other pictures of atonement. But the primary verb is "justified." The final sentence describes God the Judge as both "just" and "the justifier" of the followers of Messiah.

Yet the metaphor of God's courtroom for atonement is also not perfect. For one thing the judgment is yet future. For another, that judgment will be according to deeds done in this life (Romans 2:6–7; 14:10; 2 Corinthians 5:10; James 2:12). Thus, McKnight says about the promise of justification "Paul is declaring that the future judgment of God is reaching into time now— final eschatology is in the process of realization now" (92). It is a promise now that we will reach the future time of judgment and be found innocent.

How can people be promised now that they will be vindicated in judgment then? That is where controversy and many views compete with one another. Virtually no one thinks it means that faith in Yeshua actually perfects us so that on judgment day God will agree that we deserve to be vindicated. Let's call that idea acquittal by merit. On the other side, virtually no one believes that God's judgment ignores whether we actually believe and obey. Let's call that idea acquittal by legal fiction. In between legal fiction (God pretending we are righteous) and merit (the idea that we deserve to be called innocent) is the wide ground where truth lies. In some way, God will accept our imperfect faith, our imperfect love, and our imperfect faithfulness as a basis for acquittal.

McKnight argues that the basis for our acquittal will be that we are in Messiah (96–97). Part of what this means is being in the earthly community of Messiah (Israel and the Church) where the ways of God are practiced. Our union now with Messiah changes us and makes us part of the righteous community that will be acquitted in the final verdict. To be more specific is a mystery. Our part is to believe, to participate, and to be confident in Messiah rather than in ourselves.

Metaphor #3: Reconciliation

In the world to come when we see the great banquet table laid out before us we will catch sight of the perfect friendship of angels and men dining there. Every seat will be full and no place will be there for us. But the Master will say, "Make room at the head of the table for this one, for I wish to honor my friend." Thereupon those at the table will see us for the first time and welcome us to choice wine and delightful bread.

We are estranged from God. Reconciliation, as McKnight

says, is a metaphor in the realm of personal relations (38). God's wrath is against us. As he was being led to his cross, Yeshua said to the women mourners, "there will be great distress upon the earth and wrath against this people" (Luke 21:23, ESV). As a nation, Yeshua's own people were alienated from God and bound for a time of distress. All references in Yeshua's teaching to future judgment, to sinners being lost, to what sort of people end up accepted by God and what sort do not, have to do with estrangement and reconciliation.

In Leviticus the people were alienated from God, shut out from the Presence because they bore in their bodies guilt and death. In Yeshua's teaching, Israelites needed to repent in order to enter the kingdom that was coming. He spoke of the danger of being shut out by God in outer darkness. He dined with sinners offering reconciliation, the surprising possibility that those who had been at odds with God and God's people could return and be accepted. He said of one such sinner, "salvation has come to this house," and "the Son of Man came to seek and to save the lost" (Luke 19:9–10, ESV).

One of the functions of the sacrifices, especially the reparation offering (see chapter 7, "The Sacrifices of Leviticus") was to repair the damage done to the relationship of the worshiper to God. In the reparation offering the offenses were sacrilege, either a mistreatment of holy things or a sin against another person so grave God considered it a sacrilege against himself. The reparation offering was necessary so that the worshiper could even be allowed near to the Presence. Reconciliation with God often had a prerequisite of restitution to persons defrauded (Leviticus 5:23 which is 6:4 in Christian Bibles). Likewise acceptance before God in worship, according to Yeshua, requires first attempting to reconcile with people (Matthew 5:23–24).

Reconciliation is a metaphor used for the relationship of humans to God, of humans to each other, and even of the created order to God. Paul viewed himself as reconciled to God through Messiah and entrusted with a mission to bring that same reconciliation with God to others (2 Corinthians 5:18–20). Jews and gentiles, formerly alienated to one another, are reconciled in Messiah since they can now share the same faith (Ephesians 2:16). Creation itself is estranged from God, carrying in it death and corruption (Romans 8:21–22). Yet even the universe will be reconciled to God in Messiah (Colossians 1:20).

The result of reconciliation is friendship and sharing life together. Yeshua said, "You are my friends . . . No longer do I call you servants" (John 15:14, ESV). The banquet is laid out in the world to come: "The Lord of Hosts will make on this mount for all the peoples a banquet of rich viands, a banquet of choice wines" (Isaiah 25:6, JPS). The result of reconciliation is feasting with God and an end to estrangement from his direct Presence.

Metaphor #4: Redemption

When we see the people of that city for the first time they will appear as princes and as maidens of shining virtue, but we will know ourselves to be nothing more than servants. As we look around for the place for those of our low station a hand will grasp our shoulder from behind and the King will say, "Bring the best robes for this one, for I have redeemed this servant." And princes will bow and maidens will place flowers on our head.

Redemption is the theme of Passover, recalling how a nation of slaves was liberated and elevated by God to the status of a free people. Their status was elevated when they were redeemed from slavery. Redemption in Torah and the Hebrew Bible could refer to buying a relative out of debt slavery (Leviticus 25:47–50), redeeming (purchasing back) land or objects lost by various means (Leviticus 25:25–34; 27:9–28), avenging a murdered relative (Numbers 35), or rescuing a relative (as Boaz did for Naomi by marrying Ruth) from any kind of neediness or loss of status. So the root meanings of redemption are recovery from loss, lifting up the worth of one who has been lowered in status, and liberating from oppression.

At the Last Supper Yeshua gave hope of a new Exodus through his body and blood. He pictured himself as a redeemer and his followers as those who needed liberating. He seeks and saves what was lost. He sets at liberty those oppressed. What Mary said about God at the news of her pregnancy is also true of Messiah: he has "exalted those of humble estate" (Luke 1:52).

Paul says there is a "day of redemption" coming when our present bodies will be ennobled to a deathless perfection and that we have God's seal guaranteeing this blessing (Ephesians 4:30). It is in Messiah that we have this redemption (Ephesians 1:7; Romans 3:24). We wait eagerly for this redemption of our bodies in the coming age (Romans 8:23). What we are now is a mere shadow of what we will be. As slaves in Egypt became a free people, so we who are trapped in the corruption of death and guilt will be freed to be imperishable, glorious, powerful, and in the image of the man of heaven (1 Corinthians 15:42–49).

Redemption has already begun and in this present age Messiah's followers are given worth in him. To be in Messiah is to be adopted by God, to take on the role of a son or daughter (Romans 8:15). We have been purchased and so we should live to glorify God (1 Corinthians 6:20) and not become enslaved to anything (1 Corinthians 7:23). Redemption is pledged and sealed for the future and will be complete only when God makes us what we will be (Ephesians 4:30).

Metaphor #5: Ransom

As we ascend to the Holy One and pass the clouds our joy will be interrupted by the pull of unearthly chains, cold as ice, riveted to our hearts. We will blanch and our soaring spirit will begin to fall. A host of heaven will appear and the rider who leads it will cut our chains as angels cry, "He has ransomed a people for God." Then we will join that host and follow the rider to the city.

Concerning ransom, McKnight says, "Jesus' identification [with us] was to the point of death, being captured, as it were, by sin and death and the devil, and his powerful resurrection broke the chain of this captivity and set us free" (110). He calls ransom a "military metaphor" (38). In war nobles and important people were often spared and taken as hostages by the enemy. In this sense ransom could be very similar to redemption, a purchase to redeem a hostage. But ransom can also mean freeing captives by might and force. In Deuteronomy 7:8 (JPS) we find that the Lord "freed" Israel "with a mighty hand and rescued you from the house of bondage, from the power of Pharaoh king of Egypt." Similarly in Isaiah 35:10 (JPS) the exiles in Babylon will become "the ransomed of the Lord" and will return free from bondage "while sorrow and sighing flee." So ransom can be made by a victorious rescue as well as a payment. The common element is rescue and liberty from chains.

Yeshua ransomed by making a payment: "the Son of Man came not to be served but to serve, and to give his life as a ransom for many" (Mark 10:45, ESV). He also ransomed by defeating the evil powers. Messiah "disarmed the rulers and authorities and put them to open shame, by triumphing over them in him" (Colossians 2:15, ESV). He triumphed over death, setting us free: "the law of the Spirit of life has set you free in Christ Jesus from the law of sin and death" (Romans 8:2, ESV). Having risen from death he defeated it so that it "no longer has dominion over him" (Romans 6:9, ESV).

He has bought us out of chains and delivered us from the domain of darkness (Colossians 1:13). The realm of the enemy was invaded. But it seems in this life as if the chains still hold us. In our experience there is still death, in spite of Messiah's triumph. Thus, it is from our point of view that Paul can say death is the last enemy to be destroyed and then we will be free (1 Corinthians 15:26). We are ransomed, but we will fully experience it when all claims of evil powers and the curse are released like broken chains.

Chapter 10

The Full Picture of Messianic Atonement

When atonement is grasped in its full sense, it is liberating, enlightening. When atonement is only partially grasped it can be mocked and distorted. The following sad reductions of atonement can only be overcome by a lofty view, a wide perspective, a far-reaching apprehension.

Atonement has been called Divine Child Abuse. This is a criticism from Christian circles and formerly Christian circles. The Father is angry (supposedly) but the Son is loving. So, like some divine Pocahontas, the Son throws himself between the Father and the people of the world on whom the Father's wrath is about to be unleashed. The Father abuses the Son and spends his wrath. In this act, humanity is rescued by the Son and the Father is now willing to forgive since his anger has passed.

This notion can be described in various ways. Maybe God has multiple personality disorder (in some moments merciful and in others wrathful). Maybe God is immature and emotionally volatile like the gods of the ancient world were thought to be. Maybe atonement was an idea for a naive age in which God could be viewed in this way, but surely we have moved on.

Atonement as believed in by Yeshua's followers has been called Human Sacrifice. This is a criticism from Jewish circles. Yeshua was possibly a pious Jew who became a human sacrifice in order to appease the angry God. Or Yeshua was possibly a deceiver who believed he would continue to exist after death and erroneously offered himself like some vestal virgin to avert the evil decree. Or Yeshua was misunderstood and it was not he, but his followers, who erroneously declared him a sacrifice.

These views are reductions. As we will see, properly understood, the wrath of God is not about a divine mental problem. It is the kind of wrath we feel at a heinous act, such as harm done to children by cruel people. As we will see, the notion of Yeshua as a sacrifice is not reducible in any way to an actual sacrifice. He was not offered by worshipers seeking to appease any deity. He was not slaughtered in the fashion of either an Israelite or a Greek or Roman sacrifice.

All sacrificial talk of Yeshua's death is symbolic. Notions about God's wrath and appeasement need to be nuanced. Scot McKnight discusses three distortions common in presentations by both advocates and critics of the penal substitution theory of atonement (described below). God does not have multiple personality disorder, but his wrath is a consequence of his love. Relations between the persons of the one God are not characterized by conflict, but rather atonement is the Father's plan and also the Son's. Finally, penal substitution could never be the sole explanation of atonement (more below, and see McKnight, "Nuancing Penal Substitution," 41–43).

Understanding the all-encompassing, cosmos-healing work of Messiah will bring us to a higher level of faith and hope. We need to understand *how* Messiah accomplished atonement. How does it work? Why is it effective? Messiah accomplished six things in making atonement and they all go together into one full picture.

The Full Picture, Simply Stated

McKnight boils all the theories of atonement into one short statement: *identification for incorporation* (107). Using some of McKnight's other insights, let me expand that:

Yeshua's atonement is:

» *total identification with us*

» *all the way down to death*

» *for the purpose of incorporating us*

» *into his victory*

» *into his destiny*

» *into his people*

» *and into his redeemed cosmos-to-come.*

Another simple statement, but which is not as specific is that Yeshua died "for them, with them, and instead of them" (107). Yeshua did all this not only for the future redeemed cosmos, but also "so that they can form the new community where God's will is realized" (108).

There are myriad ways in which Yeshua identifies with Israel and with all humanity. Many threads of scripture find resolution in Messiah's atonement. For example, we might say the curse of Torah was resolved in him, poured out on him, so that Israel might be liberated from the curse (Galatians 3:13). For all humanity we might say he identified to the point of becoming "sin for us" (2 Corinthians 5:21). The ultimate penalty is death, which he took upon himself, identifying all the way down, and defeated death to set us free (Romans 6:8). The condition of human failure is sin brought about through temptation, which Yeshua also identified with, yet without sinning (Hebrews 4:15).

There are also abundant blessings into which Messiah incorporates us. We are incorporated into his victory over death and the guilt we bear for injustices done in the body. We are incorporated into his life, so that the life we now live is, in some ways of speaking, his life (Galatians 2:20). We are incorporated into his destiny, fellow heirs with Messiah of the kingdom (Romans 8:17; Daniel 7:22). Thus we inherit along with him the cosmos-to-come. Meanwhile we are incorporated into his people, his body, and the community in which atonement is worked out in this life. Changed lives and the beginnings of total healing start here and now in the body of Messiah on earth.

The accomplishments of messianic atonement have been defined in various theories. I will call them instead six accomplishments. They are all true, but only together. They all fit together, as McKnight says, into the full picture which is *identification for incorporation*. These six accomplishments overlap, but only when taken all together do they describe what atonement really is.

Accomplishment #1: Recapitulation

Only a divine Messiah can accomplish recapitulation. The concept of recapitulation is God's acquaintance with and summing up in his own experience the story of human suffering in order to raise humans above it. As McKnight says, "Jesus recapitulated Adam's life, Israel's life, and the life of every one of us" (101).

In recapitulation God entered humanity, invaded it, in order to rescue it from within. He "became what we are so that we could become what he is" (110). The Son of Man descended from the heavens to be lifted up, so that those who are in him will be glorified with him. The Servant recapitulated Israel's story, being the ideal son of Israel and lifting Israel above the curse. The Second Adam, the perfect image-bearer, came and restored the image of God in humanity.

A mere martyr could not accomplish recapitulation. A human Messiah could not, by dying, lift us up. Yeshua's accomplishment is more than a sacrifice. God is not merely appeased. Yeshua himself is an aspect of God's being, the divine man whose divinity is part of the mystery of God's differentiated being. Forever the Son was in relation with the Father, both at one and yet also differentiated from the Father. The mystery of the Son's divinity is foreshadowed in the theophanies and indwellings of the divine Presence in Israel's history. The Presence himself took on humanity, recapitulated humanity's story, and elevated humans toward divinity. As much as people can become like God, Yeshua will bring us there.

Accomplishment #2: Ransoming Victory

The divine Messiah was able to do what no one else could. He lowered himself to the form of a servant, identifying with humanity all the way down to death. He submitted to capture "as it were, by sin and death and the devil, and his powerful resurrection broke the chains of this captivity and set us free" (McKnight, 110).

Identification for incorporation is the method by which Messiah ransomed us in his victory over death and all the powers. God took on the experience of death, lived it to identify with us. He did not settle for banishing death by a mere decree. In an act of supreme love he broke it from within, as one who tasted it even as we do.

Then the ransoming victory came in the resurrection. The divine Messiah bound by the chains of death broke them. The curse on humanity, the curse on Israel, the stranglehold which the powers opposed to God held over us, were all broken.

Then our liberation from captivity came in being incorporated in Messiah. It is not that Messiah alone broke the chains, but that we were attached to Messiah (110). We died with him and we live with him. Our life is in him. Call this connection symbolism. Call it mysticism. The divine Messiah so identified with us, his intent was to include us in his victory.

Accomplishment #3: Satisfaction

McKnight says that Yeshua identified with us even down to "our sinful, guilty, God-dishonoring condition" (111). It might not seem as if Yeshua identified with our sin, except two things are true that we must remember. One, Yeshua was tempted as we are and was not an innocent like Adam in the Garden. Two, Yeshua took on humanity as we know humanity, not the ideal humanity God intended in the first man and woman. He suffered the condition of brokenness, want, and mortality just as we do.

The satisfaction theory by itself is inadequate. The theologian Anselm argued that the Son had to become one of us to argue for us before God in the divine court. At the same time only a divine representative such as the Son would be adequate to win the case. Another way to say it is that Messiah had to be truly human to experience death and truly divine to provide a sacrifice that would satisfy the whole weight of human guilt. McKnight says Anselm's theory is insufficient (111).

So in what sense did Messiah's accomplishments include satisfaction? The answer, says McKnight, is that Messiah's identification with us "is in some sense a satisfaction of what God needs for God to be given his proper glory" (111). Our punishment was experienced by Messiah. God broke the law of sin and death by taking sin and death upon himself through the divine Messiah. As McKnight says, the satisfaction theory as devised by Anselm may be "overblown," but there is "an element of satisfaction" in Messiah's identification with us. God is just in his judgment and also the justifier of all who are in Messiah, because Messiah satisfied divine justice.

Accomplishment #4: Substitution

If Messiah died with us, for us, and instead of us, it is the "instead of us" part that is substitution. Sin-guilt was on us, but Messiah took it on himself. Death was our sentence, but Messiah took it on himself. The human condition of suffering, want, and mortality was our condition, but Messiah lived it himself.

Because of Messiah's substitution for us, sin-guilt was removed like the scapegoat in Leviticus carried it away. McKnight says, "The sending of the live goat into the wilderness is explained as a substitution— represented both in the laying on of hands and the transfer of the sins onto the head of the goat" (111). God made Messiah, who was sinless, to become sin (to dwell in the condition of suffering, want, and mortality) so that we, who are the actual sinners, might become "the righteousness of God" (2 Corinthians 5:21).

By itself this accomplishment is too little to bring about the things atonement promises. Without substitution, however, Messiah's identification with us would be incomplete. He identified with us to the point of standing in our place before the Father.

Accomplishment #5: Penal Substitution

The concept of penal substitution is highly related to the concept of substitution. McKnight states the difference succinctly: "He died instead of us (substitution); he died the death that was the consequence of sin (penal)" (113). This theory, especially because this theory alone tends to be presented in some varieties of popular Christian preaching, is the one most subject to criticism. Is this the Father abusing the Son?

McKnight says the problem which led to such criticisms was failing to understand penal substitution as part of the larger picture, which is identification for incorporation: "Adam sins and the divine punishment (wrath) brings death; Jesus obeys and brings life" (113). Messiah's identification with us requires that he take the condition of judgment upon himself. Otherwise he has not identified with us completely.

More so than some idea of the Father taking his anger at us out on the Son, it is more like God in one aspect of his being chose to experience our condition. He determined to rescue us from within, fully sympathizing with us as he did so. The Father suffered in giving up the Son and in understanding the pain of the human condition. Father and Son were not at odds, but one in this resolve. No description of an angry Father pouring out abuse on the Son is accurate. A grieving Father loved us enough to give his Son and to experience the pain of loss.

Furthermore, penal substitution does not result in full atonement. As McKnight says "it only explains the wrath-to-death" problem (113). That is, penal substitution answers the question, "Why must the Son of Man die?" It does not answer the question, "How does the Son of Man bring life?"

Accomplishment #6: Representation

Representation means Messiah represents us before God. It is a category highly related to substitution on the one hand and to priesthood on the other. McKnight explains that representation means both that Messiah represents us exclusively (substitution) and inclusively (incorporating us into his destiny, victory, and people). Exclusive representation is the idea that "he dies and rises instead of us but for our benefit by incorporation" (112). To some degree a priest is a substitute, standing in our place, offering to God on our behalf. Inclusive representation means that we are included with Messiah in his death and resurrection. In various ways the people of Israel were included in the relation of the priest and the king to God. Representation is a priestly accomplishment.

McKnight sees representation in a number of biblical themes leading up to their resolution in Messiah (112). The people of Israel suffered or were rewarded to a large degree based on the rightness or wrongness before God of whatever king was on the throne at the time. The actions of the priests in the Temple represented the people, repairing relations between God and people. The Son of Man in Daniel is the divine Messiah, the one who represents humanity while being divine. The Servant in Isaiah is both Israel and the one ideal representative of all Israel, who is Messiah. The book of Hebrews makes much of the priestly, representative role of Messiah.

To represent us Messiah identified with us, being a sympathetic sharer in our condition. To restore us he incorporated us into himself, so that his death and resurrection represented our death and resurrection. To truly lift us out of our condition, he had to be a divine Messiah, able to bring us up with him beyond our human condition. No priest or king could do what Yeshua did. Only a divine priest and king could represent us as Yeshua did.

Summary

Messiah experienced and summed up our story so that we would live in him and join his glorious story. He incorporated us into his ransoming victory over the powers that held us captive. He satisfied the law of sin and death which we could never do. He died and rose instead of us, a substitute for us, so we could be incorporated into them. He died the death that is the ramification of sin-guilt. He represented us by incorporating us into his death and life. In all these things he identified with us all the way down to death for the purpose of incorporating us into his victory, his destiny, his people, and his redeemed cosmos-to-come.

Leviticus and Messiah"s Atonement

The Torah is open-ended, raising questions and revealing needs which would require some answer by God in the future. Leviticus shows a partial solution in the Temple, with the Presence indwelling the nation. Yet the greater things to come arrived in the person and work of Messiah. This is a matter of faith, in the present time, with evidence of Messiah's life, the power of his words, the eyewitnesses of his resurrection and ascension and so on.

Can we trace, from Leviticus to Messiah, something of the trajectory of need and fulfillment, question and divine answer? Are unresolved issues from Leviticus met in Messiah? Did Leviticus truly lead us to expect something like what Yeshua has done?

In Leviticus God drew near to Israel to invite Israel near to him. He became near in the indwelling Presence in the Temple. Yet he remained far off, separated from the people inside the shrine. Messiah came nearer, becoming what we are so we can become what he is. Leviticus was nearness. Messiah's atonement is more, complete identification.

In Leviticus God chose to dwell in the vicinity of sin and death to identify with Israel through the act of indwelling the nation. Messiah did more, identifying with us all the way down to death itself as the victor who ransomed us. Whereas in the Temple God had established a symbolic system to wipe away the pollution of death, Messiah did more. He broke the power of death by the resurrection.

In Leviticus we learn that God will not permit his Presence to be tainted with the pollution of human sin and death. He appointed blood for a symbolic purification. In Messiah God satisfied his honor, his separateness from sin and death symbolically in the death of Yeshua. Both Leviticus and Messiah brought symbolic satisfaction of God's desire to remain separate. Messiah's death, however, goes beyond satisfaction to incorporation of the people of faith into Messiah.

In Leviticus God had Israel send away the scapegoat as a substitute for the people. It bore sins away to the desert demons. Messiah identified with our sins in a similar way to the scapegoat, substituting for us also and symbolically removing sins. Yet unlike the scapegoat, Messiah is also able to give us life. The identification with Messiah is double: with his death and with his resurrection, which is more than the scapegoat could do.

In Leviticus animals died as a result of human transgression and as a result of corruption of human death which needed frequent purification. Messiah died also as a consequence of human sin and because human death needed to be broken. Messiah's substitution is more complete because in one act of identification the consequences of sin and death are overturned.

Finally, in Leviticus the priests represented worshipers before God's Presence. Messiah represents us as priest in a new way, incorporating us in his life so that we are lifted up with him. He is the resurrected and resurrecting priest, the incarnated divine Messiah who elevates us to a divine life. He became what we are, fully sympathizing with us. He makes us what he is, like God in the ways that people can become like God. We will be deified in the world to come, sharing God's perfect love and goodness forever. We will realize the full meaning of our sonship and daughtership through the Son.

In every way, then, Messiah's atonement takes what was revealed in Leviticus to the next chapter. All of the essential elements were symbolically present in Leviticus. They are all resolved to perfection in Messiah.

POSTSCRIPT: A Definitive Statement

Scot McKnight finds one of the most complete and enlightening biblical descriptions of atonement in a book that should come as no surprise: Hebrews (107). That statement comes in Hebrews 2:14–18, which I present here in the ESV translation. I will use superscript numbers to mark and then comment on how this statement includes much of what we have learned about atonement:

Since therefore the children share in flesh and blood, he himself likewise partook[1] of the same things, that through death[2] he might destroy[3] the one who has the power of death, that is, the devil, and deliver[4] all those who through fear of death were subject to lifelong slavery. For surely it is not angels that he helps, but he helps the offspring of Abraham. Therefore he had to be made like[5] his brothers in every respect, so that he might become a merciful and faithful high priest[6] in the service of God, to make propitiation[7] for the sins of the people. For because he himself has suffered when tempted[8,] he is able to help those who are being tempted.

1. *"Partook of the same things" is identification.*

2. *"Through death" means identification all the way down.*

3. *"Destroy" shows his ransoming victory which he incorporated us into.*

4. *"Deliver" is also about ransoming victory.*

5. *Being "made like" is identification which is necessary here for representation.*

6. *He became "a merciful and faithful high priest" repre-*

senting us by identifying with us and incorporating us in himself.

7. "Propitiation" is a sacrifice word meaning to win favor and repair separation.

8. "He himself has suffered when tempted" refers to Messiah's identification with us all the way down to our sinful condition.

Chapter 11

Yeshua's Resurrection and Leviticus

Leprosy. As a reader of science fiction and fantasy novels, my understanding of leprosy was shaped long before ever reading the Bible. Fellow geeks will recognize the name Thomas Covenant, the main character in a set of fantasy novels by Stephen R. Donaldson. When I think of leprosy, I think of the disease known by that name in modern times: Hansen's disease. A victim loses sensation, first in fingers and toes, and cannot feel injuries. Every cut and bruise is a potential infection. Thomas Covenant constantly runs through checks, looking for injuries a dozen times a day in his numbed extremities. The danger is infection leading to gangrene and removal of limbs. Think rotting fingers and toes and a colony of people miserable and outcast.

That's not what "leprosy" is in the Bible. It's a case of mistaken identity. Biblical leprosy is a skin disease. The confusion in names goes back a long way in history. The best solution, the one I learned from Jacob Milgrom's commentary on Leviticus, is to use a more accurate name for the biblical disease. It is scale disease (Milgrom 1991, page 817).

And scale disease is a miraculous condition. Its onset and healing are a negative and positive miracle. What is this biblical affliction all about? How does it point to a greater miracle: the resurrection of the body, which is total healing from death?

Milgrom notes that the Septuagint uses *lepra* to translate the biblical disease of Leviticus 13–14, which in Hebrew is *tzara'at*. But lepra is not the Greek term for leprosy as we know it today. The Greeks called that disease *elephas* or *elephantiasis* (816). The great father of medicine, Hippocrates, used the word *lepra* as a term for skin diseases. It was in the ninth century CE that the confusion in names began, when John of Damascus started referring to what is now known as leprosy or Hansen's disease by the term *lepra*. What used to be the name for skin diseases became confused with the disease of the nerve endings that is now known as leprosy. Bible readers would be confused and mistaken from this time on.

In his pursuit of medical opinion on the topic, Milgrom invited a dermatologist to address his graduate students with an appraisal of the biblical disease as described in Leviticus (817). There are three diseases of the skin which bear similarity to the symptoms described in the Bible: psoriasis (scales erupting from the skin), vitiligo (white, irregular shaped patches in the skin where the pigment has been lost), and favus (a fungus infection resulting in scaly growths).

The dermatologist said to the graduate students, however, that biblical leprosy could not be any of these conditions (817). First, none of them singly fits the biblical symptoms. Second, and most importantly, the Bible prescribes quarantine for first one week and then for a second week. The chronic skin diseases that seem comparable to biblical leprosy will not change within such a short period, much less be fully healed. In other words, medical science knows no disease like *tzara'at* (biblical leprosy, what should be called scale disease).

The onset of scale disease is miraculous, though we would say it is a negative miracle. All biblical examples of people becoming afflicted are a miraculous occurrence, such as the famous story in which Moses' sister, Miriam, was smitten with the disease (Numbers 12:10). The verb used to describe the onset of scale disease is *nega*, a word related to touch. Getting scale disease is to be touched by God with an affliction. The verb is used of smiting with disease or figuratively with divine punishments like disease on many occasions (Genesis 12:17; Exodus 11:1; 2 Samuel 7:14; 1 Kings 8:37–38; 2 Kings 15:5; Isaiah 53:4; Psalm 38:1; 89:33; 91:10).

This may not be the type of miracle anyone wants to encounter, but it is a divine touch. A disease unknown to science would fall on people suddenly. They would come before the priest to be examined (Leviticus 13:2). If the symptoms matched, the priest would quarantine them and declare them impure (13:3, 45–46).

If the symptoms partially matched, the priest would quarantine them first for a week and then a second week (13:4–5).

The implication is that some people would get a condition suspiciously like scale disease and could possibly be healed in less than two weeks. No one is healed of psoriasis, vitiligo, or favus in two weeks.

Those who fully developed the disease would be quarantined also, until they were healed. Those who were fully afflicted with scale disease were walking corpses. Until they experienced the positive miracle of healing, they lived in a perpetual state of mourning their own symbolic death. Yet when the healing came, they appeared again before the priest.

Those who experienced the negative miracle of affliction also experienced the positive miracle of healing. And the ceremony for their healing was symbolic of resurrection from the dead.

Miriam, Gehazi, Naaman, Uzziah

When Moses' sister and brother opposed him, God afflicted Miriam but left Aaron untouched. Had God afflicted Aaron, he would have been disqualified from serving as priest, had to endure quarantine, and would have had to go through purification at the hands of one of his sons. Thus, God touched Miriam with scale disease and left Aaron only to suffer sympathetically for his sister and in the knowledge that their jealous complaining together brought this condition on (Numbers 12:1–15).

Leading up to Miriam's affliction we read that Adonai's anger burned against she and Aaron (12:9). Twice in verse 10 the onset of Miriam's condition is described with a passive verb ("she was leprous"). The arrival of scale disease was sudden and inescapable. In begging Moses to forgive them and pray away the burning anger of Adonai, Aaron said, "Let her not be as one dead, who emerges from his mother's womb with half his flesh eaten away" (12:12, JPS).

To be afflicted with scale disease is to be like a corpse. There are multiple reasons for this. The whiteness is like flesh without circulation. The scaly appearance appears like rot or fungus infestation. And the flaking scales are like the skin peeling off and the body wasting away. Milgrom comments on Aaron's words in Numbers 12:12, his reference to a stillborn child, with a medical observation: "the most striking external feature of such a stillborn child is the way the superficial layers of the skin peel off" (819, Milgrom is citing a medical authority).

Miriam's affliction lasted only seven days. Again, this confirms that scale disease is not natural, but supernatural.

In 2 Kings 5, the story of Naaman the Syrian, we find a postlude about Gehazi, the servant of Elisha. While Elisha turned down an offer of great wealth from Naaman, Gehazi secretly pursued the Syrian general to obtain silver and clothing anyway. As soon as Gehazi appeared before his master, Elisha declared via supernatural knowledge what Gehazi had done and the divine punishment. In one sense the description of scale disease afflicting Gehazi is identical to that which afflicted Miriam: his disease would be "like snow" (2 Kings 5:27). Also, Miriam's crime and Gehazi's were similar: defying a prophet of God.

As for the scale disease of Naaman, there is no indication it was a punishment. Naaman was favored by Adonai even prior to meeting Elisha, as the story begins with the note: "through him the Lord had granted victory to Aram [Syria]" (2 Kings 5:1, JPS). Yet he was already a scale-diseased person (a *tzarua*). It would seem he was touched with disease by God so that he could come to a prophet in Israel and be redeemed.

In 2 Chronicles 26, Uzziah of Judah (a.k.a. Azariah in 2 Kings 15) sinned by taking for himself a prerogative of the priests in burning incense in the holy place in the Temple. The priests quoted Torah to him, "It is not for you, Uzziah, to offer incense to the Lord, but for the Aaronite priests" (2 Chronicles 26:18, JPS). Uzziah had a censer in his hand, ready to offer the incense. Then, at the very moment of his anger, before he even began to offer incense, the supernatural knowledge of Adonai was evident. Uzziah's anger alone brought on his immediate affliction: "leprosy broke out on his forehead in front of the priests in the House of the Lord beside the incense altar" (26:19, JPS).

He was rushed out of the Temple. His affliction in the Temple itself no doubt caused defilement and we can assume the priests would have proceeded with the purgation rite of Leviticus 16 (it was not just for Yom Kippur). As for Uzziah, he remained a *tzarua* the rest of his life and "lived in isolated quarters . . . cut off from the House of the Lord" (26:21, JPS). Like Miriam and Gehazi, but unlike Naaman, Uzziah's affliction was a punishment. Yet he had defied the Torah itself and the role of priests as ordained by Adonai.

These four cases all fit the theory that scale-disease is a supernatural affliction. It is usually punitive, but sometimes redemptive. The one who is afflicted is like a corpse. Sometimes the affliction was followed by healing, but sometimes it was permanent. In one case, it was even passed down to descendants.

Mourning One's Own Death

As we saw in chapter 4, all forms of ritual pollution in Leviticus and Numbers symbolize death or loss of life. Scale disease is a particularly compelling example. In Leviticus 13:45–46 we read the practices required of a *tzarua* during his or her affliction:

» *wearing only clothing that has a conspicuous tear in the fabric*

» *their hair would be unbound and allowed to grow uncut and wild*

» *he or she when encountering people would cover the upper lip*

» *he or she when encountering people would call out a warning, "Impure!"*

» *he or she would dwell in a quarantined region*

A tear in one's clothing is an ancient sign of mourning. In Leviticus 10:6, Aaron and his sons were forbidden to show signs of mourning the death of Nadab and Abihu. One of those signs was wearing clothing with a tear in it, a practice which continues in Judaism today (usually now with a piece of torn fabric pinned onto clothing).

Another sign of mourning, for Aaron and sons in Leviticus 10:6 and for the *tzarua* in 13:45, was "neglecting" their heads. Milgrom comments in both places that the issue is not merely leaving the head bare, but letting the hair go unbound and wild (608, 803).

Covering the region of the upper lip (the mustache region on men) is identified by the rabbis and Milgrom as a mourning rite, based on Ezekiel 24:17 (JPS), "Moan softly; observe no mourning for the dead: Put on your turban and put your sandals on your feet; do not cover over your upper lip." Similarly in Micah 3:7 a day is coming when prophets will cover their upper lips in mourning because there is no divine word.

The *tzarua* warns those who approach with the cry "Impure!" so that they will avoid becoming impure. There are two ways a person can become impure in the proximity of scale-diseased persons: touch, and being under the same roof or tent (Milgrom 804, 993). Milgrom demonstrates by means of Leviticus 14:8, by analogy with the case of one with a genital discharge (a *tzav*) in Leviticus 15, and by analogy with one who bears corpse impurity in Numbers 19, that a scale-diseased person could defile by touch or by being under the same roof or tent (993). They bear in their own bodies the contamination of death. This is also the reason for their quarantine, since they should not touch or be under the same roof with others. It is not forbidden to touch a scale-diseased person, but it will make one ritually impure.

So the lepers of the Bible live like those in perpetual mourning—for themselves. They are the walking dead (ritually speaking). Their case is like that of the mourners in Lamentations, during the period of mourning for the death of the city of Jerusalem:

> *They wandered blindly through the streets,*
> *Defiled with blood,*
> *So that no one was able*
> *To touch their garments.*
> *"Away! Unclean!" people shouted at them,*
> *"Away! Away! Touch not!"*
> *So they wandered and wandered again;*
> *For the nations had resolved:*
> *"They shall stay here no longer."*
> *The Lord's countenance has turned away from them,*
> *He will look on them no more.*
> *(Lamentations 4:14–16a, JPS)*

The Purification Ceremony and Resurrection

The ceremony for the purification (not healing, there is no ceremony that heals in Torah) of scale-diseased persons is abounding in symbolic meaning. In some ways it is similar to the purification of people with corpse impurity in Numbers 19, but not completely. Some rabbis and Milgrom suspect it of being comparable to a Near Eastern incantation but divested of its magical properties and given new, and strictly symbolic, meaning in Torah. The ceremony as found in Leviticus 14 contains the following elements:

» *it is only for those who have been pronounced healed by the priests*

» *two live birds (clean) are chosen*

» *cedar wood is gathered*

» *scarlet wool yarn is gathered*

» *hyssop is gathered*

» *one bird is killed (crop pulled off) over a clay vessel with fresh water*

» *the cedar, yarn, hyssop, and live bird are held by a priest*

» *they are dipped into the bloodied water*

» *the priest sprinkles seven times on the healed person using these four items in his hand*

» *he pronounces the healed person clean*

» *he releases the live bird*

» *the healed, clean person launders all clothing*

» *the healed, clean person shaves all hair*

» *the healed, clean person immerses himself/herself in water*

» *the healed, clean person must live outside of a tent or house for seven more days*

» *the healed, clean person shaves all hair, launders all clothes, and immerses again on the seventh day*

» *the healed, clean person makes offerings on the eighth day*

» *the priest anoints the offerer on the eighth day*

The cedar and scarlet (used also in Numbers 19 for the ceremony for purification of corpse impurity) are red, symbolizing blood. The hyssop plant was used for applying blood in sacrificial rites (Exodus 12:22; Numbers 19:6, 18; Psalm 51:9). The blood of one bird is mixed with fresh water, adding the life force of the bird to the water that will be sprinkled for purification. But what of the bird that is released alive?

Milgrom compares the released bird to the scapegoat from Leviticus 16: "both share the same goal: elimination of impurity" (840). What is symbolized by the impurity that is eliminated, sent away in the form of a living bird? The answer is death.

The *tzarua* was dead and is now alive, in symbolic terms. There has been a resurrection. Following a seven-day period of further cleansing (similar to the period for a corpse-contaminated person in Numbers 19) the healed *tzarua* will be able to rejoin the people in normal dwellings, once again a full member of the community. The healed, cleansed *tzarua* is alive like the bird that is released. One bird died, like the *tzarua* was dead and another is released, as the *tzarua* is released from the state of death.

"Baptism" for the Dead

A study of the ceremony of purification for a person who made contact with or was under the same roof with a corpse in Numbers 19 produces similar results. A corpse contaminated person is sprinkled with water containing symbolic elements (including the famous ashes of a red heifer). They immerse themselves on the third day and seventh day (Numbers 19:12). They are then pronounced clean.

It is no accident that the Pharisee, Paul, explaining to his non-Jewish audience in Corinth how resurrection is pre-figured in Torah and revealed further by the prophets, refers them back to Numbers 19. The problem is few readers are aware of the connection, which Paul assumes his readers will naturally make (or perhaps he has already schooled them in the mysteries of Numbers 19).

The Corinthians are skeptical that something like the bodily resurrection of the saints in Messiah could actually happen. One of the arguments Paul uses is from the authority of Torah, specifically Numbers 19: "Otherwise, what do people mean by being baptized on behalf of the dead? If the dead are not raised at all, why are people baptized on their behalf?" (1 Corinthians 15:29, ESV).

The idea of "baptizing" for the dead has sounded to some like a way to improve the lot of dead loved ones in the afterlife. Yet an idea like this would be foreign to a Pharisee and Jewish teacher like Paul. There is a much simpler explanation. "Baptize" is simply the usual Greek word adopted by Jews to describe ritual immersion. In Torah, is there a situation in which people would be immersed "for" their dead loved ones?

That is exactly what Numbers 19 says a person who touches the corpse of their loved one (or any other corpse) must do. They must come to the priests for a sprinkling ceremony and go through a seven day period of purification with two "baptisms." They endure this inconvenience of being impure and submitting to various rites "for" or on behalf of their dead. That is, in love, they must care for the corpse of those who have died, but in so doing they incur time-consuming obligations.

Paul the Pharisee saw in this Torah ceremony a hint of the mystery of life after death. Being purified after touching the dead body of a loved one is symbolic of a great hope. God does not take joy in the death of our loved ones. Their death is unclean. The God of Life does not choose death. Therefore, the logical conclusion is that he will reverse it. The ultimate meaning of purification from death-contamination is life in the presence of God in his eternal sanctuary.

Life from the Dead in Messiah

A person who had contact with a corpse needed purification, a "baptism" for the dead. A person who had scale disease was a walking corpse until healed, and then the ceremony of purification for them pictured resurrection. For those who can see it, Leviticus and Numbers point to life from the dead. These themes also point to the atonement, complete atonement, that would one day be made in Messiah Yeshua.

The slain bird in Leviticus 14 is like recapitulation, Messiah identifying with us all the way down to death. The living bird which is released is like ransoming victory, Messiah experiencing life from the dead as the forerunner of resurrection for all of us. The red heifer in Numbers 19 died to rid Israelites of the symbolic defilement of death. Messiah died and rose to ransom us completely from the actual prison of death.

Some will object that I am being too allegorical or reading things into Leviticus and Numbers that are not there. Truly these things were not completely evident before a Jewish teacher with a small following who deemed him a possible messiah was killed by the powers that be in Jerusalem. If he had remained dead, it would never have become evident. Yet he was "declared to be the Son of God in power" by his "resurrection from the dead" (Romans 1:4, ESV). And when we turn back to Leviticus and Numbers we have to ask: why did God make the condition of death central to his entire system of purity regulations? Did he not imply, by doing so, that he intended to do away with death? And if one came who was the first to break the grip of death, are we not justified in bringing these ideas together?

Chapter 12
Yeshua's Ascension and Daniel

In order for Messiah to accomplish atonement in its full sense, it was necessary for him to represent us, sharing in our condition of death and the penalty of human guilt. It was also necessary, if he was to bring us up with him and also to make a complete satisfaction, that he would be divine. This strange double requirement, which we realize only after the fact and which was not laid out in any Hebrew Bible text in advance, makes us realize all the more how uniquely wonderful it is that Messiah is human and divine.

If there is any text which foreshadows a messianic figure with a dual identity, it is Daniel 7 and the vision of the One like a son of man. In recent times an Orthodox Jewish scholar of Talmud and Second Temple Judaism, Daniel Boyarin, has argued that the notions of the New Testament that Yeshua was divine as well as human are perfectly consistent with Judaism then and now. In his book, *The Jewish Gospels: The Story of the Jewish Christ*, Boyarin makes statements such as (bracketed statements are my words):

» *"Others [Jewish thinkers in the Second Temple period] believed that God had a divine deputy or emissary or even son . . ."* (5).

» *". . . that the redemption was going to be effected by that same second divine figure mentioned above and not a human being at all. And still others believed that the two [human messiah and divine second figure] were one and the same . . ."* (5).

» *"I will show that . . . 'Son of God' referred to the king of Israel . . . while 'Son of Man' referred to a heavenly figure and no human being at all"* (26).

» *"Some Jews had been expecting this Redeemer to be a human exalted to the state of divinity, while others were expecting a divinity to come down to earth and take on human form. . . . Either way, we end up with a*

double godhead and a human-divine combination as
the expected Redeemer" (34).

» *"Daniel''s vision itself seems to require that we understand 'the one like as son of man' as a second divine
figure"* (43).

» *"A God that is far away generates—almost inevitably—
a need for a God who is closer"* (45).

» *"A second approach, currently enjoying ascendance
especially among New Testament scholars, sees the
earliest versions of high Christology as emerging
within a Jewish context"* (55).

» *"Notwithstanding later theological niceties, the Gospels also comprise a story of a God who becomes man
(theophany) and another of a man who becomes God
(apotheosis)"* (84).

» *"This is the paradox that inhabits the Gospel story of
the Christ as well: on the one hand, the Son of Man is
a divine person, part of God, coexistent with God for
all eternity, revealed on earth as the human Jesus; on
the other hand, the human Jesus has been exalted and
raised to divine status"* (90–91).

» *"The great innovation of the gospels [as opposed to
various literature of Judaism] is only this: to declare
that the Son of Man is here already, that he walks
among us"* (101).

To clarify my opinion on the matter, which Boyarin raises,
about the paradox of Yeshua being God already who became
man and yet being presented in some Gospel texts as if he was
a man becoming God, I believe this is a matter of appearance
and experience. Yeshua was the Divine Messiah who entered the
human condition through birth via Mary. Yet in the experience of
those who met Yeshua in Galilee and Judea long ago, his divinity
was veiled and only revealed mysteriously in life and apocalypti-

cally in his resurrection and ascension. As Paul said, "his Son . . . was declared to be the Son of God in power according to the Spirit of holiness by his resurrection from the dead" (Romans 1:4, with this use of "Son of God" meaning divinity, unlike its uses in the Gospels).

Yeshua's dual nature is necessary for atonement to be effective. Yeshua's dual nature is foreshadowed in the great Son of Man vision of Daniel. The Son of Man identity is something Yeshua referred to constantly in connection with himself in the Gospels. The reality that Yeshua is the Son of Man, and always was, came to his disciples by the faith-exploding impact of his resurrection and ascension. The ascension of Yeshua is not only evidence that he is the Divine Messiah, but is also part of his work as our atonement.

Throne Succession

An unrivaled monarch invests his successor, usually one of his many sons by many wives and concubines, with the symbols of power. It is a scene familiar at least in theory to many in the ancient world. And so in Daniel 7 a transcendent ruler, aged in appearance, is seen to have incomparable power:

> As I looked on,
> Thrones were set in place,
> And the Ancient of Days took His seat.
> His garment was like white snow,
> And the hair of His head was like lamb's wool.
> His throne was tongues of flame;
> Its wheels were blazing fire.
> A river of fire streamed forth before Him;
> Thousands upon thousands served Him;
> Myriads upon myriads attended Him;
> The court sat and the books were opened.

(Daniel 7:9–10, JPS)

This description is not intended to reinforce the "old man in the sky" view of God, but to compare him to an emperor understood in human terms. The divine reign over the cosmos is invisible but mighty. No emperor among humans has a throne like this and the court and servants of even great rulers cannot match Adonai's myriads upon myriads (ten thousands of ten thousands). Those with a view for heavenly things can understand that something greater than nations and armies is truly in control of human destiny. The machinations of empires will turn out to be nothing when God decides to take over all power on earth.

As Boyarin observes, however, "A God that is far away generates—almost inevitably—a need for a God who is closer" (45). Thus throughout the revealing of Adonai in Torah and prophets we find the idea of some aspects of God's being much closer to our world than God's totality. His Spirit hovered over the primeval waters in Genesis. His spoken word made the world (the Memra in Aramaic, or the Dibbur, or Logos in Greek). His Glory appeared in various forms, most often as a fiery light hidden in a cloud, in the days of Israel's wandering. His Name was said to dwell in Jerusalem. The Glory, Word, Name, Presence was always an aspect of God much closer to the people than his full godhead.

The distinction between God in his totality and the aspects of himself which he reveals to people can also be like an aging emperor (God in his totality) and his successor, a son to whom all rule and power is given (the one like a human being [Son of Man] in Daniel 7):

As I looked on, in the night vision,
One like a human being
Came with the clouds of heaven;
He reached the Ancient of Days
And was presented to Him.

Dominion, glory, and kingship were given to him;
All peoples and nations of every language must serve him.
His dominion is an everlasting dominion that shall not pass
away,
And his kingship, one that shall not be destroyed.
(Daniel 7:13–14, JPS)

Until I read a comment by Daniel Boyarin, I had never thought before of the exact significance of the description "one like a human being" (usually rendered as in the ESV "one like a son of man"). Boyarin says this young figure who approaches the Ancient of Days is "a God who looks like a human being . . . a reference to his human-appearing divinity" (33). Of course there is only one God and Daniel does not intend to show a second one. Yet this is not clarified in Daniel 7. The potentially heretical idea of two Gods is allowed to stand and it is left to the reader to grasp that "the one like a son of man" is not a separate God but the sum of all the immanent aspects of God. No theology of Father and Son being of one nature but separate persons is expounded in Daniel. The relation of Father (Ancient of Days) and Son (the one like a human being) is a mystery here.

Yeshua's Throne Succession

In Daniel 7 the one like a human being comes "with the clouds of heaven." This image of the Son of Man coming with the clouds is capable of being reinterpreted to refer to the return of Messiah, the Second Coming (Revelation 1:17). Yet its original context and meaning have to do with appearing before the throne of the Ancient of Days. "Coming with the clouds" is in its plain meaning an image of accession to the throne of cosmic power.

In the Fourth Gospel, Yeshua speaks of the Son of Man who descended from heaven (John 3:13). This Son of Man is given authority to judge the world (5:27). The Father has "set his seal" of authority on this Son of Man (6:27). He will ascend again to where he was before (6:62). People will lift up the Son of Man (on a cross, to kill him) but after this he will be truly lifted up (ascend to heaven, 8:28). The death of Yeshua is the beginning of the time at last when the Son of Man will be glorified (12:23). The crowd calling for Yeshua's arrest asks, "Who is this Son of Man?" (12:34). When Judas left to betray him, Yeshua said, "Now the son of man is glorified, and God is glorified in him" (13:31, DHE).

This theology of the Son of Man, his ascension with the clouds to appear before the Father and receive his kingship, is reflected in the story of Yeshua's ascension in Acts 1:9–11 (ESV):

> *And when he had said these things, as they were looking on, he was lifted up, and a cloud took him out of their sight. And while they were gazing into heaven as he went, behold, two men stood by them in white robes, and said, "Men of Galilee, why do you stand looking into heaven? This Jesus, who was taken up from you into heaven, will come in the same way as you saw him go into heaven."*

Luke knows his imagery, as did his audience. He carefully mentions the cloud, a hint at the true significance of the bodily ascent of Yeshua. This is not simply a translation like that of Elijah. In one strand of Second Temple Jewish thought, Enoch who "walked with God," was the Son of Man. Elijah was taken up, but not given authority. The Bible does not say that Enoch was given authority either, but a legend from Yeshua's time claims he was. In Acts 1, Luke shows who the Son of Man is. Yeshua ascends into a cloud which "took him out of their sight." The cloud seems to be acting like a chariot. The obvious implication is that Yeshua is appearing "with the clouds of heaven" to the Father.

Yeshua is able to complete atonement because he is the uncontested ruler of all the cosmos. If he incorporates us who follow him into his kingdom, his destiny, his people, then we are reconciled and redeemed. The Father invests him with dominion that will never end.

Is this something Yeshua actually claimed during his life-time? We have just seen that in the Fourth Gospel this teaching is clear. Yet many would also want to see this in the other Gospels. The well-known and much argued about Son of Man theme in Mark, Matthew, and Luke also declares Yeshua to be the Divine One who is "like a son of man."

Son of Man in the Synoptics

The literature on this subject is enormous and, though I have read a great deal of it, I will simplify and refer only to a few key ideas. There are a number of false trails on the subject of the Son of Man in Mark, Matthew, and Luke. Some think Yeshua's refer-ences to the Son of Man in the third person indicate he thought someone else was the Son of Man. Rather than argue I will simply offer an interpretation under the assumption Yeshua is indirectly claiming to be that "one like a son of man" in Daniel. If this reading is compelling, then it stands on its own.

Boyarin points out that interpreters throughout history who have ignored the Hebrew Bible background of terms like Son of Man and Son of God tend to get it exactly backwards (26). The Son of God in the Hebrew Bible is a term most specifically used of the Davidic kings, the small "m" messiahs (2 Samuel 7:14; 1 Chron-icles 17:13; Psalm 2:7). Those seen in the Gospels calling Yeshua "Son of God" mean "Davidic heir" and are suggesting he will take up the throne of Israel and begin the messianic restoration. They do not mean that he is the second member of the Trinity.

Meanwhile, some have assumed "son of man" in the Gos-pels means simply "human being." A common misunderstanding is that Yeshua, who knew he was the "Son of God" (interpreted as divine), was too humble to make that claim and called himself "Son of Man" to shrug off his followers' pretensions that he was divine. In actuality, Son of Man was an ambiguous term. Did Ye-shua mean it as in Ezekiel ("human being") or as in Daniel (the Divine One who is ""like a son of man")? Son of Man is a title in the Gospels that actually implies divinity while Son of God is not.

Boyarin points to two Son of Man sayings of Yeshua as strongly indicating the lofty identification to which that title alludes:

> . . . *the son of man has the authority to forgive sins on the earth (Mark 2:10, DHE).*

> *Therefore, the son of man is master even of the Shabbat (Mark 2:28, DHE).*

Boyarin says, "It would be very difficult to interpret the verses of Mark 2 . . . as meaning that any old human has the capacity for forgive sins against God or that any person is Lord of the Sabbath" (36). Yeshua's sayings are mysterious claims (they were mysterious when he uttered them) to be the judge of all humankind (with authority to forgive sins) and the supreme interpreter or Torah (setting principles for how Sabbath is to be observed).

The cumulative effect of the Son of Man sayings in the synoptics is to see Yeshua referring to himself all along. A strange theory that Son of Man can only mean the exalted, returning Messiah has led many to assume that the Son of Man sayings were put into Yeshua's mouth (in other words, invented) by his followers after him. Many elaborate theories propose the idea that Yeshua uttered many wisdom proverbs about sons of men (human beings) which were taken out of context by his followers and expanded into claims to divinity.

Yet the collection of Son of Man sayings taken together fits well as a fitting way for Yeshua to speak. He was reticent to make direct messianic claims which would be counter-productive. Those who claim exaltedness are usually doubted. To show is better than to tell. So the Son of Man sayings would be understood by those who saw the reality of Yeshua's exalted identity. As Boyarin puts it, "If, however, we understand that the designation Son of

Man refers not to a single stage in the narrative of Jesus—birth, incarnation, sovereignty on earth, death, resurrection, or exaltation—but to all of these together, then these problems are entirely obviated" (37–38).

The Son of Man is "like a human being" in Daniel 7. That is, there is something human about him which could be appearance only (Daniel does not address the full theology of the human and divine natures) but his true identity is divine. Yeshua is the Son of Man who descended from heaven (John 3:13). To his followers, and Boyarin argues that the Synoptic Gospels contain this theme, it seems as if he became divine in stages (apotheosis, 90–91). Yet it is also true that he was divine all along, the Divine Redeemer who descended (theophany, 90–91).

In complete agreement with the Hebrew Bible and also speculations from the Second Temple period about Messiah, he was human and divine. The ascension of Yeshua recorded in Acts 1, is his accession to the throne. As the unrivaled monarch of the cosmos, his power passed on to him from the Ancient of Days, Yeshua the Divine Messiah has authority to complete atonement and do what he has promised.

Saints in Daniel 7

Who actually possesses the kingdom in Daniel 7? Is it the One like a Son of Man or is it the Holy Ones (saints)? Both kinds of statements find their way into Daniel 7. On the one hand:

> *Dominion, glory, and kingship were given to him; All peoples and nations of every language must serve him. His dominion is an everlasting dominion that shall not pass away, And his kingship, one that shall not be destroyed. (Daniel 7:14, JPS)*

And yet, on the other hand, when Daniel asks for an explanation of what he has seen, the angelic interpreter of visions who helps him explains:

> *These great beasts, four in number mean four kingdoms*
> *will arise out of the earth; then holy ones of the Most High*
> *will receive the kingdom, and will possess the kingdom*
> *forever—forever and ever.*
> *(Daniel 7:17-18, JPS)*

So now, rather than the One like a Son of Man, it is the Holy Ones (saints) who receive and possess the rule of the land in God's age to come. When Daniel explains more detail about the fourth beast in his vision, he says:

> *I looked on as that horn made war with the holy ones and*
> *overcame them, until the Ancient of Days came and judg-*
> *ment was rendered in favor of the holy ones of the Most*
> *High, for the time had come, and the holy ones took pos-*
> *session of the kingdom. (Daniel 7:21-22, JPS)*

Again the ones who are said to possess the kingdom are the Holy Ones. Finally, the angelic interpreter explains more details about how the fourth beast, who is an eleventh king arising from a fourth kingdom, will rebel against the Most High and how the Most High will respond:

> *He will speak words against the Most High, and will harass*
> *the holy ones of the Most High. He will think of changing*
> *times and laws, and they will be delivered into his power*
> *for a time, times, and half a time. Then the court will sit*
> *and his dominion will be taken away, to be destroyed and*

abolished for all time. The kingship and dominion and grandeur belonging to all the kingdoms under Heaven will be given to the people of the holy ones of the Most High. Their kingdom shall be an everlasting kingdom, and all dominions shall serve and obey them. (Daniel 7:25–27, JPS)

So which is it? Do the saints possess the kingdom or the Son of Man? In a longstanding interpretation, many equate the two. The "one like a son of man" is a figure for "human beings." That is, some say there never was any Divine Messiah figure in Daniel 7. The description of the kingdom and unending dominion being given to the "one like a son of man" or "one like a human being" in verses 13–14 is simply a way of saying that the kingdom will be given to a certain group of human beings, who are the Holy Ones or saints.

Boyarin sees it differently. He notes that arguments from Christian church fathers going back to the fourth century long ago raised a definitive objection to the "human beings" interpretation: "Clouds—as well as riding on or with the clouds— are a common attribute of biblical divine appearances, called theophanies (Greek for 'God appearances') by scholars" (39–40).

But what does Boyarin make of the Holy Ones, who are at first thwarted by the fourth beast-king? He decides that Daniel 7 is a contradictory chapter, one in which an earlier vision (perhaps one authentically passed down from Daniel who lived in the Persian era) was taken up by a later editor (someone Boyarin thinks lived in the Maccabean era) who sought to change the meaning of the vision. He says:

The text itself seems to be a house divided against itself. The answer to this conundrum is that the author of the Book of Daniel, who had Daniel's vision itself before him, wanted to suppress the ancient testimony of a more-than-singular God, using allegory to do so. In this sense,

*the theological controversy that we think exists between
Jews and Christians was already an intra-Jewish controversy long before Jesus (43).*

Yet there is also a third way to read Daniel 7. The first way
makes the "one like a son of man" simply a strange collective
description of a group of human beings. The second way, Boyarin's, sees a contradictory reinterpretation by a later editor of an
original Divine Messiah vision by Daniel. The third way is to simply
understand the kingdom is possessed and received by both the
Divine Messiah and the saints.

Yeshua said, "In the new world, when the Son of Man will
sit on his glorious throne, you who have followed me will also sit
on twelve thrones, judging the twelve tribes of Israel" (Matthew
19:28, ESV). In Luke's version we read, "You are those who have
stayed with me in my trials, and I assign to you, as my Father as-
signed to me, a kingdom, that you may eat and drink at my table
in my kingdom and sit on thrones judging the twelve tribes of
Israel" (Luke 22:28–30, ESV). Paul, quoting what appears to be a
hymn from the early congregations, says: "if we endure, we will
also reign with him" (2 Timothy 2:12, ESV).

It seems that in the early days of the Yeshua movement,
there was an understanding that the Son of Man (Yeshua) would
receive the kingdom from the Ancient of Days (the Father) and
also give the kingdom to the Holy Ones. It is not inherently contradictory to say that King and the subjects possess the kingdom.
This is because the King rules in order to bless and share all good
things with the subjects. The good and perfect ruler to come
grants to his followers possession along with himself of the kingdom of God.

Ascension and Atonement

The divinity of Yeshua is both theophany (God descending to earth) and apotheosis (a man ascending to divinity). The

theophany side of Yeshua's identity is a well-known Christian concept. God became man. It happened via a virginal conception and an ordinary birth.

What is discussed less often is the sense in which, at the same time, Yeshua ascended into divinity. The idea of Yeshua's apotheosis is real in two respects. First, the experience of those who knew him, listened to his words, and observed his works was a realization only at the end that he was divine. In the experience of the disciples, Yeshua ascended from teacher to Messiah to the Divine Messiah, with the great revelation coming at his resurrection and then ascension. They now knew him to be far more than they understood when they left their tax stalls and fishing nets to follow him.

Second, there is a sense in which Yeshua actually ascended into his divinity. Living as a teacher in Galilee, Yeshua's divinity was veiled almost beyond recognition. Rising from the Mount of Olives to be taken up in the cloud to the throne of the Most High, Yeshua's divinity was revealed in full. The Divine Messiah gave up the prerogatives of divinity such as omnipotence and omniscience and omnipresence to identify with us and become perfected as a servant all the way to death. Had he remained so veiled and limited in his powers, we could guess that full atonement could not have been made.

Yet when he ascended to be taken up in the cloud, this was no longer the limited servant who could be in only one place. This was no longer the Son of Man who could be killed. This was no longer the Son who had limited knowledge of mysteries and depended on the Father and Spirit for special revelations while he was among us. Now this was the Divine Messiah with his full powers restored, ascending to claim his eternal kingdom. And so the ascension of Messiah is a necessary component of our full atonement, which extends beyond all time and rises above all merely human improvement programs. The One like a Son of Man received his kingdom and will give it to us, his followers, to possess for all time.

Chapter 13

Yeshua as the Servant in Isaiah

"My servant shall prosper, be exalted and raised to great heights," God said in Isaiah (52:13, JPS). At times the Servant speaks in his own voice, "He hid me in the shadow of his hand, and he made me like a polished arrow" (49:2, JPS). At times the Servant is clearly a collective term for a group, "Jacob My servant, Israel whom I have chosen" (44:1, JPS). At times the individuality of the Servant could not be more obvious: "It is too little that you should be my servant in that I raise up the tribes of Jacob and restore the survivors of Israel: I will also make you a light of nations" (49:6, JPS).

"Servants" in Isaiah exist on three levels. First, all among the people of Israel are called to be "servants" of Adonai. Second, the righteous remnant within larger Israel (and also righteous gentiles) are actually carrying out their role as "servants" of Adonai. Yet, third, the description of an individual Servant, someone more than a collective figure, more than "all Israel" and greater even than "all the righteous," stands out in Isaiah.

The three levels of meaning of "servant" confuse readers, but it should be remembered that Isaiah is a many-layered book full of mysteries and rarely makes its symbolism easy for readers. It was for Isaiah and those who followed after him in writing the collection of prophecies we call Isaiah to envision ideal mysteries without explaining. In fact, it is doubtful that Isaiah or the prophets who followed him understood specifics about the idyllic visions they saw.

Why does Isaiah's servant theme matter for a book on Yeshua as our atonement? It is because some of the language of atonement figures prominently in Isaiah 53. It is also because the relationship between the One Servant and the multiple servants in Isaiah perfectly demonstrates the relationship between Yeshua as our atonement and the community of Yeshua as the continuation of Yeshua's atoning work. Let me make that more plain.

There is one who achieves atonement but many who spread it to others and give it through love to those who must receive it. As Scot McKnight indicated in the very title of his book, *A Community Called Atonement*, the community of the faithful spreads the actual realization of atonement practically into people's lives. Likewise, in Isaiah, God alone saves, but people are brought into the fold of the righteous by the community of faithful servants who are, in fact, offspring of the One Servant. The Servant is one and his offspring are servants under him. The One Servant atones and the many servants spread that atonement to others in community.

One-Dimensional Interpretation of the Servant

Who is the Servant in Isaiah? One extreme is the either-or way of interpreting Isaiah's rich imagery. It must be either X or Y. The Servant must be "all Israel" or "Yeshua." The Servant must be Moses or David, Isaiah or the righteous remnant of Israel, Hezekiah or Yeshua, and the list goes on. The either-or way of looking at Isaiah not only does not hold for the Servant passages (summarized below), but it doesn't hold for many of Isaiah's other visions.

Isaiah's visions in general are rich, with levels. Redemption is certain, but any individual's inclusion in that redemption is not. Disaster is certainly coming, but God has mercy and may relent. Adonai's house (the Temple) is a blessing for Judah, but all nations are invited. Rescue will certainly come, but the time is not yet. God will restore Israel, but also the coastlands and ends of the earth. Adonai loves Israel, but has both enemies and servants within the beloved people. Given the poetic lushness of Isaiah, can the Servant passages be one-dimensional?

Meager Interpretation of the Servant

A comparable error in interpreting the Servant theme is meagerness, ignoring or downplaying lofty descriptions of the

Servant. Talk of death and revivification must be about the historical ups and downs of the Jewish people. The exaltation of the Servant could be nothing more than a renewed people in an ideal age. The suffering to heal others could be the psychological impact of humanity repenting of war.

But Isaiah's vision is monumental, cosmos-changing. To interpret such a vision as merely a slight improvement in the human condition, to regard it as exaggeration or embellishment, is miserly and unworthy of Adonai. The Servant theme must include the bringing together of Israel and the nations, the vindication of the righteous in the divine court, the healing of death and guilt, the reconciling of God and humanity. The new thing Adonai is doing will be greater than psychological growth, than a people at peace, than a nation rescued repeatedly from oblivion. The vision of the Servant encompasses the Day of Judgment and the blissful union of all things under God"'s kingship.

The Servant Passages

» *Isaiah 41:8-16. Speaker: God. Israel is Adonai's Servant, called and chosen. God supports and vindicates Israel against her enemies.*

» *Isaiah 42:1-9. Speaker: God. The Servant will establish justice in the nations, be gentle with the weak, give sight to the blind, and bring about the new blessings God is promising.*

» *Isaiah 42:18-20. Speaker: God. Jacob-Israel is Adonai's deaf, blind, and unknowing Servant.*

» *Isaiah 44:1-5. Speaker: God. Jacob-Israel is Adonai's Servant and the Spirit be poured out on their future offspring.*

» *Isaiah 44:21-28. Speaker: God. Adonai calls Jacob-Israel, his Servant, to return, and has called Cyrus the Persian to bring it about.*

» *Isaiah 48:16b*. Speaker: Servant. The Servant speaks, saying Adonai has sent him along with the Spirit.

» *Isaiah 49:1–6*. Speaker: Servant. Called from birth, the Servant despairs, until Adonai reaffirms his mission. He will glorify God, cause Jacob to return to faithfulness, regather Israel, and bring Adonai's light and salvation to the whole earth.

» *Isaiah 49:7–9a*. Speaker: God. The deeply despised Servant will be exalted and will free prisoners.

» *Isaiah 50:4–9*. Speaker: Servant. The Servant speaks, saying that Adonai teaches and enables him to teach. He submits to tormentors knowing Adonai will vindicate him.

» *Isaiah 50:10–11*. Speaker: God. Adonai instructs the people to obey the Servant or walk in darkness. He says people cannot be saved by their own light.

» *Isaiah 52:13–15*. Speaker: God. Adonai declares that his Servant will be greatly exalted, to the befuddlement of kings and nations.

» *Isaiah 53:1–10*. Speaker: Israel. Israel speaks, declaring ignorance that this lowly, suffering Servant was actually their source of healing and redemption. They declare that he will see offspring and prolong his days.

» *Isaiah 53:11–12*. Speaker: God. Adonai speaks, promising that his Servant's anguish will lead to sight, declaring that the Servant has vindicated many in the divine court, and promising to exalt him.

» *Various references to "servants" and "offspring" in chapters 56–66*. Speaker: various. Adonai's servants are contrasted with his enemies within the people of Israel. Servants are not limited to Israelites, but specifically include gentiles. Servants are the offspring of the Servant from 53:10.

Collective Israel as the Servant

All Israel is to bring God's blessing and light to the world. To Abraham God said, "in your offspring shall all the nations of the earth be blessed" (Genesis 22:18, ESV). To Israel at Sinai God said, "you shall be to me a kingdom of priests and a holy nation" (Exodus 19:6, ESV). God says Israel is "my Servant . . . whom I have chosen" (Isaiah 41:8, ESV).

What is Israel chosen for? Isaiah does not specify, but behind the concept of Israel as servant lays the concept in Torah that Israel houses the Presence of Adonai in its shrine and serves him there (worships, the word in Hebrew originally meant "serve" and came to mean "worship"). Similarly, the idea of Israel as the light-bearer and blessing-bringer of Adonai must inform what Isaiah means by "servant." By being the people of God, the bearers of his Presence, Israel is to spread Adonai''s Glory to the ends of the earth.

Beyond Collective to the One

In the Servant passages of Isaiah, anytime the task of spreading light to the nations or being a vehicle of redemption is mentioned, one other than collective Israel seems to be in view. The one who will establish "justice in the earth" will also be "a covenant for the people" (42:6, ESV). The people are Israel, so the Servant is other than Israel.

The one of whom God says, "you are my Servant, Israel," is called to "bring Jacob back to him, that Israel might be gathered to him" (49:5, ESV). While the Servant is, in one sense, Israel, the Servant is at the same time one other than Israel whose task is to return Israel.

God repeats his promise to the Servant, that he will be "a covenant to the people" (49:8, ESV). He will apportion the land in the new era of Israel's restoration and bring the prisoners out.

In 50:10 God asks who obeys the voice of his Servant and

implies that all who do not are walking in darkness. The passage preceding this is a first-person account of one gifted by God to teach, one taught by Adonai, who suffers abuse but who submits to it with faith in God's vindication (50:4–9). The voice must be that of the Servant, since this testimony of faith is immediately followed by God's question.

In Isaiah 52:14, properly translated without emending the "you" to "him" as some versions do, there is a comparison between Israel and the Servant that forces the reader to understand the Servant transcends Israel. "Just as many were appalled at you," says God, ". . . so shall he sprinkle many nations; kings shall shut their mouths because of him" (52:14–15, ESV). If we follow the common practice of accepting an emendation of "startle" for "sprinkle," the comparison is even more clear: just as the world was appalled by Israel's exaltation, so the glorification of the Servant will startle kings.

In 53:1–10 the people of Israel are speaking. They declare an initial ignorance about this Servant, whose lowliness and suffering made him seem insignificant and low-born. Yet they came to understand he suffered in complete innocence and even vicariously. He was actually a healing of the nation's guilt, a redeeming figure best understood by the metaphor of a sacrifice of atonement. Though his death and burial were shameful, the people declare that he will see offspring, prolong his days, and bring about God's will.

God speaks in verses 11–12, declaring that the Servant's anguish will end with sight restored. This is because the Servant's act of sacrifice will cause many to be vindicated in the Divine Judgment. He has borne their guilt himself along with its punishment. As the section began with God's declaration the Servant would be exalted, so it ends with the same idea: God promises to allot to him the many and divide his reward with the mighty.

In summary, God has a Servant who restores Israel, attracts the gentiles to God, is initially despised, is revealed as a redeemer, who brings God's ways of justice to all the peoples of earth, who is taught by God, who submits to his tormenters with faith in Adonai's vindication, whose deeds bring justification in the divine judgment, who is a sacrifice satisfying divine judgment, who has offspring, and who will be high and lifted up.

The Offspring of the Servant

The Servant has offspring: "If his soul appoints a guilt offering, he will see offspring; he will prolong [his] days" (Isaiah 53:10, my translation). The multi-layered Servant theme in Isaiah comes to its high point in 52:13–53:12. Prior to that, the plural phrase "servants of Adonai" does not occur. All references to Adonai's Servant are singular until after Isaiah 53. Then, suddenly, a string of references begins to appear to Adonai's servants (plural) and to offspring. The scroll of Isaiah has a deliberate arrangement of prophecies building up visions of present faith and future hope.

The plural "servants" starts showing up in Isaiah 54:17. This new theme, of the Servant's offspring who are servants, fits with one Isaiah has been building up all along. Beleaguered Jerusalem in the days of Ahaz and Hezekiah, at times under siege and all but desolate, has a glorious future. Future Zion (Jerusalem glorified) will be secure, prosperous, and a place of true justice and exultation. Yet this glory-to-come will not be enjoyed by all, but only by the remnant of the faithful, the community of the devoted ones within Israel (and beyond Israel).

The "servants" in the last part of Isaiah are that community. No weapon can prosper against Future Zion and the servants of Adonai will enjoy it (54:17). In chapter 63, a humiliated Jerusalem after the exile (walls crumbled, Temple burned) begs God to act now. The leading voices in this prayer are the servants of Adonai (63:17). Jerusalem is debased and low, but God will preserve it for a glorious future. He will do this for the sake of his servants (65:8–9). There are still, even after the lesson of the exile, wicked ones in Jerusalem. They will not survive to see Future Zion in the New Heavens and Earth, but the servants of Adonai will enjoy its fruitfulness and peace (65:13–15). The offspring of Jacob, an allusion to the Servant's offspring from 53:10, will find delight in Future Zion (65:23). In that time of splendor and greatness the servants of Adonai will know his power (66:14).

The Servant atones, redeems. The faithful who are atoned for and redeemed carry the work forward. Their faith, hope, and deeds pass on the vision of prophets and kings to future servants. Atonement comes from a center, from Messiah, and radiates out like rays of light through the community that is atoned (as in the title of Scot McKnight's book).

The Offspring of Yeshua

Mark 10:45 (DHE) says, "For even the son of man did not come in order to be served, but rather to serve and to give his life as a ransom for the many." The saying is paralleled in Matthew 20:28. Yeshua comes to serve and ransom. Is this the Servant of Isaiah who gave his back to the smiters (50:4) and who vindicates the many by bearing their guilt (53:11)?

Some doubt the genuineness of the saying. It is clear that the early followers of Yeshua picked up on the Servant theme in Isaiah as background for understanding his identity. The early hymn of the Yeshua movement (Philippians 2:5–11) draws heavily on Isaiah 52:13–53:12. Because of a number of comparisons between the Servant and Yeshua in the New Testament, some interpreters suspect Yeshua's followers, and not Yeshua, of making the original connection.

Yet Yeshua did have much to say about servants and Mark 10:32–45 makes a strong connection between Yeshua's death and the role his disciples must play after him. They too must be servants. The reign of God will come to earth first through a suffering Messiah and then through a serving community of his spiritual offspring, says Yeshua in Mark 10:32–45. It is like the connection between the Servant in Isaiah and the Servant's offspring:

» The Son of Man will be abused and killed (Mark

10:33–34).

» The Servant was abused (Isaiah 50:4), despised (53:3–4), and killed (53:5–11).

» Many in Yeshua's day longed for eschatological (end times) glory (Mark 10:35–37).

» Throughout Isaiah all of Judah and Jerusalem hope for Future Zion.

» Yeshua asks if those who desire future glory are willing to suffer and be faithful (Mark 10:38–39).

» Throughout Isaiah the faithful remnant is encouraged through times of suffering.

» Yeshua says the glorious future can only go to those for whom it is ordained (Mark 10:40).

» Isaiah says Future Zion will be enjoyed by Adonai's servants only.

» No servant is greater than his master and the Son of Man's disciples must become slaves (disciples) to all (Mark 10:41–44).

» The Servant in Isaiah 53:11 has offspring who imitate him as servants of Adonai (54:17; 63:17; 65:8–9, 13–15, 23; 66:14).

» The Son of Man serves and gives his life a ransom for many (Mark 10:45).

» The Servant justifies the many (Isaiah 53:11), bearing guilt and appointing [himself] a guilt offering.

Yeshua's offspring will suffer like him and must serve like him. No servant will be greater than his master (John 15:20). Yeshua purifies his servants (John 13:8–10) just as the Servant in Isaiah became healing and peace to his offspring (53:5). So Yeshua's disciples, his offspring, will need to wash feet and become slaves to all just as Yeshua has done (John 13:12–16).

"A disciple is not exalted above his *rav*, nor a servant above his master" (Matthew 10:24, DHE). So Yeshua's disciples are to be like him (10:25). Yeshua opened the way and his servants are sent out to imitate him, making the way of Yeshua a reality for many. Disciples imitate the master and make disciples (Matthew 28:19–20). The Servant in Isaiah is high and lifted up. To Yeshua the Father has given all authority in heaven and in the earth (Matthew 28:18). From this authority the Servant sends out servants.

Chapter 14

In Messiah: The Reconciling of All Things

As I am writing this a hickory tree outside my window keeps attracting my attention, its golden leaves in full sunshine on this autumn day awake some hidden desire in my soul. I think about changing colors and falling leaves as the nights become colder and winter approaches. There is an idea of a coming world without death, a world where all is life. But autumn and winter happen to be things I love even though winter represents a dying. In the fully atoned cosmos, the universe to come in which all things are unified with God, will a joy like golden leaves disappear? Will it be a world without winter, one of perpetual warmth and unchanging green? These golden hickory leaves seem like the kind of beauty I would imagine being there.

In my imagination, which is continually filled with worlds of faerie like Middle Earth and Narnia, I can picture many kinds of beauty. I find a desire in myself crying out for an unblemished place, treading soft carpets of brown leaves in a tranquil wood. I can imagine deep valleys with hospitable houses beside clear rivers nestled in imposing mountains of great beauty. The world as I wish it would be is not a place of sadness, of competition with losers and winners, of acquisition with haves and have-nots. Part of the human experience is imagining a better world or better worlds. And many of us believe that one will come.

I have a thousand questions about what such a world could be. When I pray the *Aleinu* and say the words, "Adonai will be ruler over the whole earth, and on that day, Adonai will be One, and his name will be One," I wonder what it will look like. The vision for a unified creation under God in the *Aleinu* comes from Zechariah 14:9. This is ultimately what the word "atonement" means, all things being "at one" with God. Although that is not what the usual biblical words for atonement mean (they mean cleansing, wiping clean, purifying), nonetheless this is a biblical idea. Full atonement is more than simply the mechanics of cleansing, more than just a God-devised plan to do away with human guilt. It is all things becoming One with the desire of God.

Paul says of Yeshua that he is working "to reconcile to himself all things, whether on earth or in heaven, making peace" (Colossians 1:20). He says God's purpose is for the unfolding of ages of time (this present age and the coming age) "to unite all things in him, things in heaven and on earth" (Ephesians 1:10). The cosmic powers which imprison and frustrate the cosmos, which for now hold back the realization of God's desire for a perfect universe, will be defeated (Ephesians 6:12). These cosmic powers do not actually constrain God, but the mystery of redemption includes allowing this present age to be a ruin. God leaves room for evil to work itself out. But the time of evil will end and God will realize his desire for his universe in his time to come.

At the center of God's desire, the pivotal figure in bringing about all the good which God can imagine in his perfect universe, is Messiah. God will unite all things in him. When Adonai does take over rule of all things in heaven and earth, when he makes all things One, it will be through Messiah Yeshua.

Desire: Real or Unreal?

Are our desires real or not? Even the least imaginative person lives with a certain ideal about what the world should be. Upon encountering injustice, every person feels the world should be a place where such things could never happen. Similarly we imagine a world where children don't suffer from leukemia, where women are not trafficked as sex slaves, where floods don't leave people homeless, and so on.

We desire not only changes, things we would leave out from this world in the one to come, but we desire to see a continuation and heightening of some things in this world. That time laughing with friends at a warm table comes to an end sooner than we want it to. That music we enjoy carries us to heights such that we can imagine higher highs. That beach we vacation at gives us an idea of an even more blessed shore.

People have dreamed up many mythical worlds, realms of gods, and faerie universes, with a different but not baseless idea of mystery, of magic, of wonderful things hidden in the unknown. J.R.R. Tolkien wrote in his famous essay "On Fairy Stories" about how people naturally enjoy the imaginative escape of dwelling mentally on such worlds. He argued that prisoners are not morally required to think exclusively about jailers and prison walls. Our desires, in some common core we find in them from person to person, are liberating.

We either assume that there is something "real" about our desires, about the basic commonalities of our imaginations of an ideal world, or that they are simply projections of some kind. We must ask ourselves, however, where our imagination and desires come from. C.S. Lewis argued in his book *Miracles* that the mind cannot be explained simply by nature (by mere molecules, reactions on the chemical and electrical levels). If our thought-life, our reason, is nothing more than the operation of our physical brain, then nothing we think has any more significance than photosynthesis. What power do our thoughts have to be "true," to give us any window at all into reality, if they are only what we experience from reactions across the synapses of our nervous system? If our brains are formed by irrational causes (a mindless process of nature evolving) how can they produce reason?

To paraphrase Lewis, sooner or later we must consider the possibility that there is a mind whose desires exist absolutely on their own, not derived from any other source. Perhaps such a mind exists, and my mind derives through a long chain of influences from his thoughts, so that my desires also derive way back from his desires. Is it not possible that desires we humans experience are related causally to the desires of God, whose thoughts have long ago originated our thoughts? Perhaps our desires are real.

Desires: Good and Bad

Of course many desires are evil. A grasping would-be acquirer of things desires more and more, leaving little or nothing for others. Our appetite for taking can be endless. A profligate libertine can desire more sexual escapades with more partners than is physically possible. As harmless and enjoyable a thing as food is for many a slow-working poison ingested in quantities too large to be sane.

There are good desires. That moments of love should never end, that the simple joy of food and drink should linger, that an undiscovered country of unbounded beauty should be found, are all righteous cravings. We see the good in another person and wish the world contained more such. We experience a morning like no other and wonder why the others have to be so dull in comparison. We taste the unparalleled Cabernet and lament every cheap libation we ever wasted our taste buds on.

It could be that there are core ideas in our desires that are all good. Maybe free and unfettered access to any number of sexual partners is a desire that is twisted rather than inherently evil. It may be the desire for a pleasure that truly lasts, for a reversal of the law of diminishing returns in many of life's pleasures. If only every sip of cold lemonade could taste as good as the first one after we've mowed the lawn on a hot day. Maybe greedy acquisition is a desire for security or a world where we don't need security. It could be that unscrupulous cravings are simply to virtuous desires what shadows are to well-lit objects: distorted projections of the real thing.

Derived from God

If it happens that our minds derive in some sense from God, from the mind which exists absolutely on its own, then our desires could be related to God's desires. If we think of the mind of God, limitless and elaborate, we can only begin to imagine his desires. What God imagines is within his power to bring it to pass.

Could there be a world that will be according to God's desires completely? The real question is the opposite: could it possibly be that the world will never be as God desires it? The One greater than whom none exists will surely be able to make it so.

Then we can take our desires as a clue, a partial indication, of what will come. Atonement is that concept we are defining as God bringing all things into unity with his imagination and vision. He will be One and his Name will be One. All things will be reconciled and united through the agency of the One he appointed to bring about the times, Messiah.

Prophetic Glimpses

It may not exactly fit many people's model of afterlife bliss, but a repeated picture in the prophets is an agricultural heaven. Perhaps the leading image is that of each person having a secure "vine and fig tree." Though strange to moderns whose lives are more about online social exchanges and watching instant movies via the internet, it seems ancient Near Easterners really loved their grapevines and fig trees. In one biblical story an Assyrian psych-ops officer promised the inhabitants of Jerusalem if they surrendered to Sennacherib they would all have their vine and fig tree (Isaiah 34:4, like the politician's promise of a chicken in every pot). Micah, from the same era as Isaiah and Sennacherib, shot back with a promise from God: "every man shall sit under his grapevine or fig tree with no one to disturb him" (Micah 4:4, JPS). Zechariah turned the image into one of a shared feast with friends: "In that day, declares the Lord of hosts, every one of you will invite his neighbor to come under his vine and under his fig tree" (Zechariah 3:10, ESV).

Many of the prophetic glimpses of the world to come have this agricultural edge to them. I have no doubt some people find them hard to appreciate. Will the world revert to some agricultural lifestyle in those days? If so, we can imagine it will be agriculture without effort, easy fruit without irritations and hardships. Figs and wine sustained people in the ancient world and perhaps they will again. The arbor and shade of our own fig tree and flowering vine of the best grapes is a picture of abundant security and provision. The agricultural-heaven images keep piling on:

» *Vine and fig tree: Joel 2:22; Micah 4:4; Zechariah 3:10.*

» *Hills dripping wine: Joel 3:18; Amos 9:13.*

» *Plowman overtakes reaper: Amos 9:13.*

» *Adonai's banquet: Isaiah 25:6.*

» *Blooming desert, growing forest: Isaiah 32:15; 35:1–2, 6–7; 51:3; 58:11.*

» *Trees, healing, living water: Ezekiel 47.*

» *Raising grain, blossoming: Hosea 14:7.*

There are many other aspects of Final Age bliss hinted at in the prophets. The quickest of summaries must include:

» *Undoing divisions between Israel and the righteous of the nations: Isaiah 2:2–4; Micah 4:1–3; Zechariah 9:9–10.*

» *The globe governed by Torah ideals: Isaiah 2:2–4; Micah 4:1–3; plus Isaiah 42:4; 60:9; 66:19; Ezekiel 37:24.*

» *The globe covered by knowledge of Adonai: Isaiah 11:9; Habakkuk 2:14.*

» *Circumcised hearts, new hearts: Deuteronomy 30:6; Jeremiah 31:33; Ezekiel 36:26.*

» *Resurrected bodies: Isaiah 26:19; Ezekiel 37; Daniel 12:2.*

» *Messiah and justice: Isaiah 11:1–5; Jeremiah 23:5–6; 30:21–22; 33:15; Ezekiel 37:24; Daniel 7:13–14.*

» *End of death: Isaiah 11:6–9; 25:7–8.*

» *Dwelling of people with God: Isaiah 24:23; 25:6; Jeremiah 3:17; Ezekiel 37:26–28; 48:35; Micah 4:6–7.*

» *Healing: Isaiah 35:5–6; 61:1–4.*

Some of the prophetic glimpses suggest a temporary age of bliss, especially Isaiah 65:17–25. There is no clear differentiation between a coming golden age, the days of Messiah, and a final age of unending bliss. The lines are blurred and a consistent theology is not the goal. Other examples of the promises suggest an unending, new state of things. Some have called this "telescoping," like a view from far away in which the observer cannot distinguish distances. What they saw with great hope was God breaking in, the foolish reigns of men coming to an end, and a better world and a glorified humanity.

It is a mistake to limit atonement to individual forgiveness for sin. As Paul said, "creation waits with eager longing for the revealing of the sons of God" (Romans 8:19, ESV). The world has been subjected to "futility" (Romans 8:20), but it will be liberated. The entire universe is waiting for atonement. Atonement ultimately means all of God's desires, for us and for his universe, coming to pass, and doing so freely and without coercion.

The Realization of Desire

What was implied in Torah, what is poetically elaborated in prophets like Isaiah, was more fully contemplated by those who came to the realization that Yeshua is more, so much more, than he at first appeared to be. More than an activist for an Israelite revival of Torah, more than a forerunner of a golden age, more even than a heavenly Messiah set to restore Israel and the nations, the apostles contemplated Yeshua as the one in whom the entire universe would be restructured. The mystery of death and cosmic powers of decay would be resolved and the new mystery of a remade cosmos, one with heavenly matter and spiritual bodies, descriptions of a new kind of existence, would subsume. The Son of Man will reconcile all things, whether on earth or in the heavens beyond all human knowing.

After all, the ancient wisdom writers expressed the hope well: "The desire of the righteous will be granted" (Proverbs 10:24,

ESV). The Psalmist echoes this: "He will give you the desires of your heart" (Psalm 37:4, ESV). In a futuristic promise, Jeremiah said to Judah: "His desire shall be satisfied on the hills of Ephraim and in Gilead" (50:19, ESV). What desires? They are the desires deep in our psyche, translated from unworthy cravings to the purest intent in them. They are the desires of the creator of all thought and the source of longing in every human heart, the One who will unify all things. Our profoundest desires are a clue to what atonement will ultimately look like. It will all be granted and the study of atonement is a look into the process by which it has happened, is happening, and will happen.

Made in the USA
Lexington, KY
10 May 2015